Uromastyx as pets

Uromastyx Facts and Information.

Uromastyx Care, Behavior, Diet, Interaction, Costs and Health.

By

Ben Team

Table of Contents

About the Author

The author, Ben Team, is an environmental educator and author with over 16 years of professional reptile-keeping experience.

Ben currently maintains www.FootstepsInTheForest.com, where he shares information, narration and observations of the natural world.

Foreword

Uromastyx are some of the most unusual lizards in the world. While they have a rather typical body plan for a lizard, they feature unusually shaped heads, fantastic color patterns and one of the most intimidating tails found in the modern world.

These unusual adaptations are very important for the survival of these lizards, and they've helped them to thrive for millions of years in some of the harshest environments on the planet. And for several of the species that make up the Uromastyx genus, this includes the Sahara Desert.

Because they live in such unforgiving habitats and have such a unique set of tools at their disposal, they also exhibit several behavioral adaptations that distinguish them from other lizards even further. For example, uromastyx exploit a few food sources that few other lizards do, and they exhibit well-defined tunneling behaviors, which, while not unheard of, are fairly uncommon among other lizards.

This combination of traits – including their unique appearance, lifestyle and behavior -- combine to make these lizards very popular among reptile enthusiasts. Many of whom love the otherworldly nature of these species.

But despite hailing from such distant lands, uromastyx can make excellent pets for those who are prepared to provide them with the habitat and resources they require. But in order to understand the proper way to keep these lizards in captivity, you'll have to understand their physiology, biology, behavior, habitat and ecology, among other things.

You can begin learning these things on the following pages. We'll delve into the world of the uromastyx, and learn how these lizards make their way in the world. And, more importantly, how you can provide them with the things they need to thrive.

With sufficient effort on your part, you can enjoy healthy and happy uromastyx for years to come. But you must begin your journey by learning all you can about them.

PART I: THE UROMASTYX

Properly caring for any animal requires an understanding of the species and its place in the natural world. This includes digesting subjects as disparate as anatomy and ecology, diet and geography, and reproduction and physiology.

It is only by learning what your pet is, how it lives, what it does that you can achieve the primary goal of animal husbandry: Providing your pet with the highest quality of life possible.

Chapter 1: Uromastyx Description and Anatomy

Aside from their unusual, spiky tails, uromastyx have the same basic body plan that most other lizards do. Like many other members of the Family Agamidae – the evolutionary lineage to which they belong -- uromastyx have stocky bodies, large heads and a sprawling body posture.

However, despite these similarities, uromastyx display several physical differences from their relatives, making it easy to distinguish them from other agamids.

Size

Although the 14 described Uromastyx species vary slightly in terms of size, most hatch out of their eggs at 3 to 4 inches (7 to 10 centimeters) in length, However, Egyptian uromastyx (*Uromastyx aegyptia*) may be slightly larger – up to 6 inches (15 centimeters) – when they hatch.

Most hatchlings weigh between 5 and 10 grams, but here again, Egyptian uromastyx may be slightly larger.

Male Egyptian uromastyx occasionally reach 30 inches (76 centimeters) in length (females are smaller), but most uromastyx species are smaller and mature at lengths of 10 to 18 inches (25 to 45 centimeters).

Most uromastyx have mature weights of 8 to 20 ounces (250 to 600 grams), but large male Egyptian uromastyx may weigh 2 pounds or more (900 grams).

Color and Pattern

Uromastyx are highly variable lizards; as a group, they exhibit a kaleidoscope of colors and patterns. This makes it somewhat difficult to describe the colors of this group of lizards succinctly.

Uromastyx color varies at both the species and individual level. Even individuals exhibit varying colors and patterns. When warm and relaxed, most uromastyx adopt their boldest, most colorful colors; when stressed or cold, their colors become quite muted.

Additionally, males and females are sexually dimorphic with respect to color. The males of most species tend to have bold colors, while females are typically clad in earth tones.

Despite the difficulties involved in characterizing the colors of this group of lizards, one thing is certain: Many species and populations possess very attractive colors, and some individuals are simply breathtaking to behold.

As a group, their colors range from brown, gray, cream and black to turquoise, blue, gold and red. Some lizards are primarily clad in two colors, while others display a rainbow of colors. The boldest colors of uromastyx typically occur on the back, head and tail, with the legs and belly being primarily earth tones.

Markings are often present along the back and other portions of the lizard's body. These may take the form of bands, jagged lines, webbing or ocelli.

Body
Uromastyx have squat, rounded bodies. The skin covering their body is relatively rough, and it often appears somewhat baggy. This loose skin allows uromastyx to expand and flatten their bodies.

This flattening behavior can help to facilitate water collection, but they most commonly use it when basking in the sunshine or attempting to dissuade predators or rivals.

Head

The heads of uromastyx are rather blocky, but the tip of the snout does come to a definitive point. Small scales cover the head, and large jaw muscles are present, which give the impression of "cheeks."

They have medium sized eyes, which are located on the sides of the head. A distinct ridge lies above each, which partially shades the eye from the sun and offers some protection from injury.

The eyes feature muscular eyelids, which can open and close at will. The skin around the eyes occasionally bears bold colors, but the irises are typically brown to yellow.

Uromastyx also possess primitive organ on the tops of their heads. Called the parietal eye, the organ resembles a discolored scale. Its primary purpose is to collect light and relays the information to the lizard's pineal gland.

However, despite being called an "eye," this organ cannot resolve images as typical eyes can. It is primarily important for informing a lizard's basking decisions and behavior, although it can likely detect the shadow cast by an approaching predator too.

The triangular tympanum (eardrum) of uromastyx is visible on the rear portion of the side of the lizard's head. However, the various folds of skin found in the region and the lizard's large jaw muscles often obscure it.

Uromastyx have rather small, inconspicuous nostrils, located on either side of the animal's snout. The nostrils often contain crusty, salt-like deposits around the opening.

Uromastyx have relatively small mouths for their size, and they don't have the expansive gape that characterizes some of their close relatives, such as bearded (*Pogona vitticeps*) and frilled dragons (*Chlamydosaurus kingii*).

Uromastyx (like most other agamid lizards) have acrodont, rather than pleurodont dentition. This means that their small triangular teeth attach to the upper surface of the jaw bones. The front of the jaw comes to a sharp point, which gives uromastyx a somewhat rodent-like appearance.

Uromastyx teeth change over the course of their life, to reflect the dietary shift that occurs with age.

Limbs and Feet

Like most other tetrapods, uromastyx have four muscular legs which lie along the sides of the lizard's body. Their legs are capable of supporting their bodies above the ground, but they usually exhibit a sprawling posture.

Five toes adorn each of their four feet. Uromastyx have long, curved nails, which extend from the tip of each toe. These nails help them to grip the substrate and climb rough objects.

Vent

The vent is a transverse opening located under the base of a uromastyx' tail, slightly behind the rear legs. This forms the exit point for all reproductive structures and products (eggs), as well as the end products of the digestive and renal systems.

The vent usually remains closed, and opens slightly when the lizards defecate, release urates, copulate or deposit eggs.

Tail

Uromastyx have long, thick tails that are covered in very hard, sharp scales. Many of the scales actually have thorn-like tips that are sharp enough to break the skin.

While these tails are clearly not prehensile, uromastyx do have strong control over them. In fact, the tails are used as a club for deterring predators.

The tail usually drags behind the body when a uromastyx moves. Uromastyx do not jettison their tails, as some other lizards do. Those who lose their tails (in whole or in part) are not capable of regenerating them.

Internal Organs

The internal anatomy of uromastyx differs relatively little from that of other lizards or tetrapods in general.

Uromastyx draw oxygen in through their nostrils; pipe it through the trachea and into the lungs. Here, blood exchanges carbon dioxide for oxygen, before it is pumped to the various body parts via the heart and blood vessels.

While the hearts of uromastyx feature only three true chambers (two atria and a single ventricle), a septum keeps the ventricle divided at most times, allowing the heart to operate similarly to a four-chambered, mammalian heart. This means that in practice, uromastyx keep their oxygenated and deoxygenated blood relatively separate in the heart.

Their digestive system is comprised of an esophagus, stomach, small intestine, large intestine and a terminal chamber called the cloaca. The stomach has some ability to stretch to accommodate food.

The liver resides near the center of the animal's torso, with the gallbladder sitting directly behind it. While the gallbladder stores bile, the liver provides a number of functions relating to digestion, metabolism and filtration. Kidneys, which lie almost directly behind the lungs, filter wastes from the lizard's bloodstream.

Like other lizards, uromastyx control their bodies via their brain and nervous system. Their endocrine and exocrine glands work much as they do in other vertebrates.

Reproductive Organs

Like all squamates, male uromastyx have paired reproductive organs, called hemipenes. When not in use, males keep their hemipenes inside the bases of their tails. When they attempt to mate with a female, they evert one of the hemipenes and insert it into the female's cloaca.

The paired nature of the male sex organs ensures that males can continue to breed if they suffer an injury to one of the hemipenes. This paired arrangement also allows male uromastyx to mate with females on either side of their body.

Females have paired ovaries, which produce ova (eggs), and they have paired oviducts, which store the eggs after they are released from the ovaries. The eggs are shelled and held inside the oviducts until it is time to deposit the eggs. At this time, the eggs are passed from the oviducts into the cloaca and out of the body via the vent.

Chapter 2: Uromastyx Biology and Behavior

Uromastyx exhibit a number of biological and behavioral adaptations that allow them to survive in their natural habitats.

Shedding

Like other scaled reptiles, uromastyx shed their old skin to reveal new, fresh skin underneath. However, they do not shed their skin in one piece, as most snakes do. Instead, uromastyx tend to shed in several separate pieces over the course of a day or two.

Some uromastyx may consume their shed skin, but this is not as common a phenomenon as it is in some other lizards, such as geckos.

Metabolism and Digestion

Uromastyx are ectothermic ("cold-blooded") animals, whose internal metabolism depends on their body temperature. When warm, their bodily functions proceed more rapidly; when cold, their bodily functions proceed slowly.

This also means that the lizards digest more effectively at suitably warm temperatures than they do at suboptimal temperatures. Their appetites also vary with temperature, and if the temperatures drop below the preferred range, they may cease feeding entirely.

A uromastyx body temperature largely follows ambient air temperatures, but they also absorb and reflect radiant heat, such as that coming from the sun. The lizards try to keep their body temperature within the preferred range by employing behaviors that allow them to adjust their temperature.

For example, uromastyx bask to raise their temperature when they are too cool. This typically involves orienting their body so that they are perpendicular to the sun's rays. Additionally, some individuals may exhibit darker colors during the early portion of the basking period (although they often adopt lighter, bolder colors once they heat up) or flatten their bodies to help absorb more infrared rays.

By contrast, when it is necessary to cool off, uromastyx may move into the shade, venture underground or gape their mouths to release excess heat.

Growth Rate and Lifespan

Uromastyx have a relatively modest growth rate. Although the rate of growth varies according to a litany of factors – including species, sex, food availability and health – most uromastyx mature in about 4 years.

There is also a great deal of variation in individual growth rates – even among siblings in the same clutch. Some clutchmates will usually grow more quickly than their siblings will. This can lead some individuals to reach twice the size of their siblings within a few months' time.

Little is known about the lifespan of wild-living uromastyx. However, they can likely live for at least 15 years. However, as with most other small to medium-sized lizards, many probably perish at the hands of predators before reaching their first birthday.

Foraging Behavior

Uromastyx forage actively for food and they ambush passing insects when the opportunity arises. Uromastyx primarily rely on their vision to locate prey and edible plants, but they may taste potential food items (particularly plant-based foods) with their fleshy tongue before consuming them as well.

Diel and Seasonal Activity

Uromastyx are almost entirely diurnal animals, who spend their days basking in the sun, foraging for food, seeking mates and defending themselves from predators.

With the onset of night, most uromastyx retreat to a burrow, where they will sleep until dawn. Some individuals may instead sleep in rock crevices or other sheltered locations.

Because uromastyx live across a very broad geographic area, they exhibit a variety of different seasonal rhythms and patterns. However, most will become inactive in regions with a defined winter period.

Defensive Strategies and Tactics

Crypsis is the first method by which uromastyx seek to defend themselves. The combination of their complex color patterns, flattened body and sedentary behavior makes them blend in quite well in their natural habitats.

When crypsis fails, uromastyx may elect to flee, usually in the direction of their burrow or some other type of cover. Once there, they will attempt to wedge their body into the crevice or tunnel, with their weapon-like tail serving as a shield.

If the predator is not deterred, or the uromastyx is caught on open ground, the lizard will swing the tail back and forth like a club. Although this behavior doesn't look particularly menacing, the sharp spines on the tail can easily cause minor injuries. Predators with delicate snouts are wise to leave uromastyx in peace.

Uromastyx rarely bite in defense, although they may void the contents of their cloacas if picked up or attacked.

Reproduction

Uromastyx exhibit varying reproductive approaches, although the variation between the various species is generally rather limited. Most species produce clutches of eggs numbering between 4 and 25, although the majority of uromastyx clutches likely number between 10 and 20.

Breeding behaviors usually begin in the early spring, shortly after the lizards emerge from their winter refuges. Males usually maintain and defend a small territory surrounding their burrows, although females and hatchlings may occasionally do the same.

Males will usually attempt to breed with any females that pass through their territory. But because females do not always acquiesce to such advances, these encounters often appear violent. Males may repeatedly bite the females to hold them in place.

Over the course of a breeding season, males may mate with several females. Females may mate with more than one male, but they can likely retain the sperm from a single mating and deposit multiple clutches of eggs over the course of the breeding season.

South Saharan Uromastyx (Uromastyx flavifasciata)

As the time for egg deposition nears, the females excavate a small egg chamber in the soil, often at the base of a shrub or rock. Once completed, the female will turn around and deposit her eggs.

The female will cover the egg chamber upon completing parturition. Once she leaves, she will have no further contact with the young. Uromastyx provide no care for the hatchlings.

Chapter 3: Classification and Taxonomy

Scientists currently recognize 14 different species (one of which is divided into two subspecies) within the genus Uromastyx.

Like all other living species, uromastyx are placed within a hierarchical classification scheme.

Kingdom: Animalia

Phylum: Chordata

Class: Reptilia

Order: Squamata

Family: Agamidae

Genus: *Uromastyx*

The species are listed below, along with their common names (not all species have a widely accepted common name).

It is important to recognize that the classification of uromastyx is not well-resolved. Different authorities recognize different species, and the individual species are often quite difficult to distinguish.

Additionally, several of the species who were formerly placed in the genus *Uromastyx* have been moved to the genus *Saara*. This primarily includes those species that are found east of Iran.

However, a reasonable list of the currently recognized species is as follows:

- *Uromastyx acanthinura* – Bell's uromastyx

- *Uromastyx aegyptia* – Egyptian uromastyx

- *Uromastyx alfredschmidti* – Schmidt's uromastyx

- *Uromastyx benti* – Bent's uromastyx

- *Uromastyx dispar* – Sudan uromastyx

    - *Uromastyx dispar flavifasciata*

    - *Uromastyx dispar maliensis* – Mali uromastyx

- *Uromastyx geyri* – Saharan spiny-tailed uromastyx

- *Uromastyx macfadyeni* – Macfadyen's uromastyx

- *Uromastyx nigriventris* – No common name

- *Uromastyx occidentalis* – Giant uromastyx

- *Uromastyx ocellate* – Eyed uromastyx

- *Uromastyx ornata* – Ornate uromastyx

- *Uromastyx princeps* – Princely uromastyx

- *Uromastyx thomasii* – Oman uromastyx

- *Uromastyx yemenensis* – Yemen uromastyx

Note that uromastyx also go by the common names mastigure, dabb lizard and spiny-tail lizard.

Chapter 4: The World of the Uromastyx

Uromastyx range across a wide geographic area and inhabit a number of different habitats throughout this range. But they are all relatively similar in several key ways.

Range

As a group, Uromastyx are found throughout the Northern Africa, including Morocco, Western Sahara, Mauritania, Algeria, Mali, Niger, Chad, Sudan, Ethiopia, Eritrea, Egypt, Lybia and Somalia.

Heading eastward, they are also found in Saudi Arabia, Yemen, Oman, Iraq, Syria, Israel and Iran.

Historically, several species of lizards in Afghanistan, Pakistan and India were also identified as uromastyx. However, these lizards have been reassigned to the genus *Saara* in recent years, effectively reducing the range of uromastyx.

Climate and Habitat

The climate and habitats found throughout this range vary quite widely. Some of the regions feature very high temperatures all year long, but most of the areas within the uromastyx' range experience distinct seasonal climates.

Typically, the temperatures are very high in the summer, cold in the winter and relatively dry throughout most of the year. Most of the rains that occur in the range of the uromastyx fall over a relatively short period of time. The timing of these rains varies from one location to the next.

Uromastyx generally prefer arid habitats, such as deserts, near deserts, scrublands and dry grasslands. However, some live in more humid, coastal zones.

Status in the Wild

The status of uromastyx in the wild is not well understood. This occurs in part because of the difficulties in identifying individuals and the precise ranges of the various species.

However, the IUCN Red List considers most of the uromastyx that have been assessed to be of "Least Concern."

Exceptions include the Egyptian uromastyx and Oman uromastyx, which are classified as "Vulnerable," as well as Schmidt's uromastyx and *Uromastyx shobraki* – which some authorities consider a separate species from the closely related eyed uromastyx. Both of these species are considered "Near Threatened."

PART II: UROMASTYX HUSBANDRY

Once equipped with a basic understanding of what uromastyx *are* (Chapter 1 and Chapter 3), where they *live* (Chapter 4), and what they *do* (Chapter 2) you can begin learning about their captive care.

Animal husbandry is an evolving pursuit. Keepers shift their strategies frequently as they incorporate new information and ideas into their husbandry paradigms.

There are few "right" or "wrong" answers, and what works in one situation may not work in another. Accordingly, you may find that different authorities present different, and sometimes conflicting, information regarding the care of these lizards.

In all cases, you must strive to learn as much as you can about your pet and its natural habitat, so that you may provide it with the best quality of life possible.

Chapter 5: Uromastyx as Pets

Uromastyx can make rewarding pets, but you must know what to expect before adding one to your home. This includes not only understanding the nature of the care they require but also the costs associated with this care.

Assuming that you feel confident in your ability to care for a uromastyx and endure the associated financial burdens, you can begin seeking your individual pet.

Understanding the Commitment

Keeping a uromastyx as a pet requires a substantial commitment. You will be responsible for your pet's well-being for the rest of its life. Uromastyx can be long-lived animals, and you must be prepared to care for your new pet for many years.

Can you be sure that you will still want to care for your pet several years in the future? Do you know what your living situation will be? What changes will have occurred in your family? How will your working life have changed over this time?

You must consider all of these possibilities before acquiring a new pet. Failing to do so often leads to apathy, neglect and even resentment, which is not good for you or your pet uromastyx.

Neglecting your pet is wrong, and in some locations, a criminal offense. You must continue to provide quality care for your uromastyx, even once the novelty has worn off, and it is no longer fun to clean the cage and prepare the vegetables he needs each week.

Once you purchase a uromastyx, its well-being becomes your responsibility until it passes away at the end of a long life, or you have found someone who will agree to adopt the animal for you. Unfortunately, this is rarely an easy task. You may begin with thoughts of selling your pet to help recoup a small part of your investment, but these efforts will largely fall flat.

While professional breeders may profit from the sale of uromastyx, amateurs are at a decided disadvantage. Only a tiny sliver of the general population is interested in reptilian pets, and only a small subset of these are interested in keeping uromastyx.

Of those who are interested in acquiring a uromastyx, most would rather start fresh, by *purchasing* a small hatchling or juvenile from an established breeder, rather than adopting your questionable animal *for free.*

After having difficulty finding a willing party to purchase or adopt your animal, many owners try to donate their pet to a local zoo. Unfortunately, this rarely works either.

Zoos are not interested in your uromastyx, no matter how pretty he is. He is a pet with little to no reliable provenance and questionable health status. This is simply not the type of animal zoos are eager to add to their multi-million-dollar collections.

Zoos obtain most of their animals from other zoos and museums; failing that, they obtain their animals directly from their land of origin. As a rule, they do not accept donated pets.

No matter how difficult it becomes to find a new home for your unwanted uromastyx, you must never release non-native reptiles into the wild.

Additionally, released or escaped reptiles cause a great deal of distress to those who are frightened by them. This leads local municipalities to adopt pet restrictions or ban reptile keeping entirely.

The Costs of Captivity

Reptiles are often marketed as low-cost pets. While true in a relative sense (the costs associated with dog, cat, horse or tropical fish husbandry are often much higher than they are for uromastyx), potential keepers must still prepare for the financial implications of uromastyx ownership.

At the outset, you must budget for the acquisition of your pet, as well as the costs of purchasing or constructing a habitat. Unfortunately, while many keepers plan for these costs, they typically fail to consider the on-going costs, which will quickly eclipse the initial startup costs.

Startup Costs

One surprising fact most new keepers learn is the enclosure and equipment will often cost as much as (or more than) the animal does (except in the case of very high-priced specimens).

Prices fluctuate from one market to the next, but in general, the least you will spend on a healthy uromastyx is about $100 (£74), while the least you will spend on the *initial* habitat and assorted equipment will be about $50 (£40). Replacement equipment and food will represent additional (and ongoing) expenses.

Saharan Uromastyx (Uromastyx geyri)

Examine the charts on the following pages to get an idea of three different pricing scenarios. While the specific prices listed will vary based on innumerable factors, the charts are instructive for first-time buyers.

The first scenario details a budget-minded keeper, trying to spend as little as possible. The second example estimates the costs for a keeper with a moderate budget, and the third example provides a case study for extravagant shoppers, who want an expensive uromastyx and top-notch equipment.

These charts are only provided estimates; your experience may vary based on a variety of factors.

Inexpensive Option

Wild-Caught Uromastyx	$100 (£74)
Economy Homemade Habitat	$50 (£38)
Light Fixtures and Bulbs	$50 (£38)
Plants, Substrate, Hides, etc.	$20 (£15)
Infrared Thermometer	$35 (£27)
Digital Indoor-Outdoor Thermometer	$20 (£15)
Water Dish, Food Dishes, Spray Bottles, Misc.	$20 (£15)
Total	**$295 (£222)**

Moderate Option

Captive Bred Uromastyx	$300 (£220)
Premium Homemade Habitat	$100 (£76)
Light Fixtures and Bulbs	$50 (£38)
Plants, Substrate, Hides, etc.	$20 (£16)
Infrared Thermometer	$35 (£27)
Digital Indoor-Outdoor Thermometer	$20 (£16)
Water Dish, Food Dishes, Spray Bottles, Misc.	$20 (£16)
Total	**$545 (£409)**

Premium Option

Adult Uromastyx Colony	$1000 (£735)
Premium Commercial Cage	$500 (£383)
Light Fixtures and Bulbs	$50 (£38)
Plants, Substrate, Hides, etc.	$20 (£15)
Infrared Thermometer	$35 (£27)
Digital Indoor-Outdoor Thermometer	$20 (£15)
Water Dish, Food Dishes, Spray Bottles, Misc.	$20 (£15)
Total	**$1,645 (£1,228)**

Ongoing Costs

The ongoing costs of uromastyx ownership primarily fall into one of three categories: food, maintenance and veterinary care.

Food costs are the most significant of the three, but they are relatively consistent and somewhat predictable. Some maintenance costs are easy to calculate, but things like equipment malfunctions are impossible to predict with any certainty. Veterinary expenses are hard to predict and vary wildly from one year to the next.

Food Costs

Food is the single greatest ongoing cost you will experience while caring for your uromastyx. To obtain a reasonable estimate of your yearly food costs, you must consider the number of meals you will feed your pet per year and the cost of each meal.

The amount of food your uromastyx will consume will vary based on numerous factors, including his size, the average temperatures in his habitat and his health.

As a ballpark number, you should figure that you'll need about $5 (£4) per week – roughly $250 (£191) per year -- for food. You could certainly spend more or less than this, but that is a reasonable estimate for back-of-the-envelope calculations.

Veterinary Costs

While you should always seek veterinary advice at the first sign of illness, it is probably not wise to haul your healthy uromastyx to the vet's office for no reason – they don't require "checkups" or annual vaccinations as some other pets may. Accordingly, you shouldn't incur any veterinary expenses unless your pet falls ill.

However, veterinary care can become very expensive, very quickly. In addition to a basic exam or phone consultation, your uromastyx may need cultures, x-rays or other diagnostic tests performed. In light of this, wise keepers budget at least $200 to $300 (£160 to £245) each year to cover any emergency veterinary costs.

Maintenance Costs
It is important to plan for both routine and unexpected maintenance costs. Commonly used items, such as paper towels, disinfectant and topsoil are rather easy to calculate. However, it is not easy to know how many burned out light bulbs, cracked misting units or faulty thermostats you will have to replace in a given year.

Those who keep their uromastyx in simple enclosures will find that about $50 (£40) covers their yearly maintenance costs. By contrast, those who maintain elaborate habitats may spend $200 (£160) or more each year.

Always try to purchase frequently used supplies, such as light bulbs, paper towels and disinfectants in bulk to maximize your savings. It is often beneficial to consult with local reptile-keeping clubs, who often pool their resources to attain greater buying power.

Myths and Misunderstandings
Unfortunately, there are many myths and misunderstandings about uromastyx and reptile-keeping in general. Some myths represent outdated thinking or techniques, while other myths and misunderstandings reflect the desires of keepers, rather than the reality of the situation.

Myth: *Uromastyx will only grow to the size of their enclosure, and then they stop growing entirely.*

Fact: Despite the popularity of this myth, healthy uromastyx do not stop growing until they reach their mature, adult size. Keeping a uromastyx in a small cage is an inhumane practice that will only lead to a stressed, sick animal.

Myth: *Uromastyx are reptiles, so they are not capable of suffering or feeling pain.*

Fact: While it is important to avoid anthropomorphizing, or projecting human emotions and motivations to non-human entities, reptiles – including uromastyx – feel pain. There is no doubt that they can experience pain and seek to avoid it. While it is impossible to know exactly what a uromastyx thinks, there is no reason to believe that they do not suffer similarly to other animals, when injured, ill or depressed.

Myth: *All you have to feed a uromastyx is crickets.*

Fact: Many uromastyx relish crickets and other insects, but these types of animal-based foods should only be offered sparingly. The bulk of a uromastyx diet should be comprised of leafy green vegetables.

Myth: *Uromastyx are adapted to temperature extremes, so it is not necessary to use a thermometer or monitor the cage temperatures.*

Fact: Uromastyx have evolved a wide array of adaptations that allow them to survive where few other animals can. However, much of the way they do this is by becoming inactive when temperatures are not conducive to activity. Uromastyx still require temperatures within a fairly narrow range, and as the keeper, you must monitor the habitat temperatures often to ensure the health and well-being of your pet.

Myth: *My uromastyx likes to be held so he can feel the warmth of my hands.*

Fact: In truth, your uromastyx may tolerate being held, but it probably does not "like" it. This myth springs from the notion that because reptiles are "cold-blooded," and they must derive their heat from external sources, they must enjoy warmth at all times. However, this is an oversimplification of their behavior.

Myth: *Uromastyx are good pets for young children.*

Fact: While many reptiles, including uromastyx, make wonderful pets for adults, teenagers and families, they require more care than a young child can provide. The age at which a child is capable of caring for a pet will vary, but children should be about 10 to 12 years of age before they are allowed to care for their own uromastyx. Parents must exercise prudent judgment and make a sound assessment of their child's capabilities and maturity. Children will certainly enjoy pet reptiles, but they must be cared for by someone with adequate maturity. Additionally, it is important to consider the potential for young children contracting salmonella and other pathogens from the family pet.

Myth: *If you get tired of a uromastyx, it is easy to find a new home for it. The zoo will surely want your pet; after all, you are giving it to them free of charge! If that doesn't work, you can always just release it into the wild.*

Fact: Acquiring a pet uromastyx is a very big commitment. If you ever decide that your pet no longer fits your family or lifestyle, you may have a tough time finding a suitable home for it. You can attempt to sell the animal, but this is illegal in some places, and often requires a permit or license to do legally.

Zoos and pet stores will be reticent to accept your pet – even at no charge – because they cannot be sure that your pet does not have an illness that could spread through their collections. A zoo may have to spend hundreds or thousands of dollars for the care, housing and veterinary care to accept your pet uromastyx, and such things are not taken lightly.

Some people consider releasing their uromastyx into the wild if no other accommodations can be made, but such acts are destructive, often illegal and usually a death sentence for the uromastyx. Uromastyx are not adapted to the habitats of North America or Western Europe. They will have very little chance of surviving, and even if they do, they will never reproduce.

Even if you live in the uromastyx' natural range, captive animals should never be released into the wild, as they can spread pathogens that may wipe out a native population. You will likely have to solicit the help of a rescue group or shelter devoted to reptiles in finding a new home for an unwanted pet.

Acquiring Your Uromastyx
Modern reptile enthusiasts can acquire uromastyx from a variety of sources, each with a different set of pros and cons.

Pet stores are one of the first places many people see uromastyx, and they become the de facto source of pets for many beginning keepers. While they do offer some unique benefits to prospective keepers, pet stores are not always the best place to purchase a uromastyx; so, consider all of the available options, including breeders and reptile swap meets, before making a purchase.

Pet Stores

Pet stores offer a number of benefits to keepers shopping for uromastyx, including convenience: They usually stock all of the equipment your new uromastyx needs, including cages, heating devices and food items.

Additionally, they offer you the chance to inspect the uromastyx up close before purchase. In some cases, you may be able to choose from more than one specimen. Many pet stores provide health guarantees for a short period, which provide some recourse if your new pet turns out to be ill.

However, pet stores are not always the ideal place to purchase your new pet. Pet stores are retail establishments, and as such, you will usually pay more for your new pet than you would from a breeder.

Additionally, pet stores rarely know the pedigree of the animals they sell, and they will rarely know the uromastyx' date of birth or other pertinent information.

Other drawbacks associated with pet stores primarily relate to the staff's inexperience. While some pet stores concentrate on reptiles and may educate their staff about proper uromastyx care, many others provide incorrect advice to their customers.

It is also worth considering the increased exposure to pathogens that pet store animals endure, given the constant flow of animals through such facilities.

Reptile Expos

Reptile expos offer another option for purchasing uromastyx. Reptile expos often feature resellers, breeders and retailers in the same room, all selling various types of uromastyx and other reptiles.

Often, the prices at such events are quite reasonable and you are often able to select from many different uromastyx. However, if you have a problem, it may be difficult to find the seller after the event is over.

Breeders
Because they usually offer unparalleled information and support to their customers, breeders are generally the best place for most novices to shop for uromastyx. Additionally, breeders often know the species well and are better able to help you learn the husbandry techniques necessary for success.

The primary disadvantage of buying from a breeder is that you must often make such purchases from a distance, either by phone or via the internet. Nevertheless, most established breeders are happy to provide you with photographs of the animal you will be purchasing, as well as his or her parents.

Selecting Your Uromastyx
Not all uromastyx are created equally, so it is important to select a healthy individual that will give you the best chance of success.

Practically speaking, the most important criterion to consider is the health of the animal. However, the sex, age and history of the uromastyx are also important things to consider.

Health Checklist
Always check your uromastyx thoroughly for signs of injury or illness before purchasing it. If you are purchasing the animal from someone in a different part of the country, you

must inspect it immediately upon delivery. Notify the seller promptly if the animal exhibits any health problems.

Avoid the temptation to acquire or accept a sick or injured animal in hopes of nursing him back to health. Not only are you likely to incur substantial veterinary costs while treating your new pet, you will likely fail in your attempts to restore the uromastyx to full health. Sick animals rarely recover in the hands of novices.

Additionally, by purchasing injured or diseased animals, you incentivize poor husbandry on the part of the retailer. If retailers lose money on sick or injured animals, they will take steps to avoid this eventuality, by acquiring healthier stock in the first place and providing better care for their charges.

As much as is possible, try to observe the following features:

- **Observe the uromastyx' skin.** It should be free of lacerations and other damage. Pay special attention to those areas that frequently sustain damage, such as the tail, the toes and the front of the face. A small cut or abrasion may be relatively easy to treat, but significant abrasions and cuts are likely to become infected and require significant treatment.

- **Gently check the uromastyx' crevices and creases for ticks.** Avoid purchasing any animal that has ticks. Additionally, you should avoid purchasing any other animals from this source, as they are likely to harbor parasites as well.

- **Examine the uromastyx' eyes, ears and nostrils.** The eyes should not be sunken, and they should be free of discharge. The nostrils should be clear and dry – lizards with runny noses or those who blow bubbles are likely to be suffering from a respiratory infection.

- **Gently palpate the animal and ensure no lumps or anomalies are apparent**. Lumps in the muscles or abdominal cavity may indicate parasites, abscesses or tumors.

- **Observe the uromastyx' demeanor**. Healthy uromastyx are aware of their environment and react to stimuli. When active, the animal should calmly explore his environment. Avoid lethargic animals, which do not appear alert.

- **Check the uromastyx' vent**. The vent should be clean and free of smeared feces. Smeared feces can indicate parasites or bacterial infections.

- **Check the uromastyx appetite**. If possible, ask the retailer to feed the lizard a green leaf or a cricket. A healthy, suitably warm animal should usually exhibit a strong food drive, although failing to eat is not *necessarily* a bad sign – the uromastyx may not be hungry.

The Age
Hatchling uromastyx are very fragile until they reach about one month of age. Before this, they are unlikely to thrive in the hands of beginning keepers.

Accordingly, most beginners should purchase two- or three-month-old juveniles, who have already become well established. Animals of this age tolerate the changes associated with a new home better than very young specimens do. Further, given their larger size, they will better tolerate temperature and humidity extremes than smaller animals will.

The Sex

Unless you are attempting to breed uromastyx, you should select a male pet, as females are more likely to suffer from reproduction-related health problems than males are.

Some females will produce and deposit egg clutches upon reaching maturity, whether they are housed with a male or not. While this is not necessarily problematic, novices can easily avoid this unnecessary complication by selecting males as pets.

Quarantine

Because new animals may have illnesses or parasites that could infect the rest of your collection, it is wise to quarantine all new acquisitions. This means that you should keep any new animal as separated from the rest of your pets as possible. Only once you have ensured that the new animal is healthy should you introduce it to the rest of your collection.

During the quarantine period, you should keep the new uromastyx in a simplified habitat, with a paper substrate, water bowl, basking spot and a few hiding places. Keep the temperature and humidity at ideal levels.

It is wise to obtain fecal samples from your uromastyx during the quarantine period. You can take these samples to your veterinarian, who can check them for signs of internal parasites. Always treat any existing parasite infestations before removing the animal from quarantine.

Always tend to quarantined animals last, as this reduces the chances of transmitting pathogens to your healthy animals. Do not wash quarantined water bowls or cage furniture with those belonging to your healthy animals. Whenever possible, use completely separate tools for quarantined animals and those that have been in your collection for some time.

Always be sure to wash your hands thoroughly after handling quarantined animals, their cages or their tools. Particularly careful keepers wear a smock or alternative clothing when handling quarantined animals.

Quarantine new acquisitions for a minimum of 30 days; 60 or 90 days is even better. Many zoos and professional breeders maintain 180- or 360-day-long quarantine periods.

Chapter 6: Providing the Captive Habitat

In most respects, providing your uromastyx with a suitable captive habitat entails functionally replicating the various aspects of the habitat he'd experience in the wild.

In addition to providing your pet with an enclosure, you must provide the animal with the correct thermal environment, appropriate humidity, substrate, and suitable cage furniture.

The first thing you must decide upon when planning how to house your uromastyx is whether you want to keep him indoors or outdoors.

Outdoor Caging

There are a variety of reasons why uromastyx are well-suited for outdoor habitats.

Almost all diurnal lizards – including uromastyx -- benefit from basking in the unfiltered sunlight of outdoor enclosures and the larger amount of space they usually afford. Additionally, by keeping them outside, you do not have to purchase expensive lighting systems. Uromastyx will also benefit from the numerous wild weeds and plants that may grow right in their cage.

However, outdoor maintenance does have a few drawbacks. Outdoor maintenance is not appropriate for all climates, and your local climate must be relatively similar to that which they experience in the wild.

In order to maintain uromastyx outdoors, your local climate must satisfy the following conditions:

- The ambient daily temperatures must reach the high-80s Fahrenheit (30 to 32 degrees Celsius) for several hours per day, for most of the year.

- The sunlight should be strong enough to produce basking spots with surface temperatures of at least 105 degrees Fahrenheit (40 degrees Celsius) for at least two or three hours per day.

- The climate cannot be excessively humid – uromastyx require moderately low humidity levels.

- The nighttime temperatures must not drop below about 65 to 70 degrees Fahrenheit (18 to 21 degrees Celsius).

If your local climate is not warm enough, additional heating elements can be added to the habitat, but if it is difficult to overcome the challenges presented by climates that are too hot.

If you do not live in an area with a suitable climate for consistent outdoor maintenance, you may be able to utilize outdoor caging for part of the year. If this is not feasible, it is still very beneficial to take your uromastyx outside for regular "walks" in which the lizard can bask in natural sunlight.

In addition to the local climate, several other criteria must be met in order to successfully maintain uromastyx outdoors.

- Pesticides, herbicides, fertilizers and other chemicals must not be used in proximity to the habitat. Because groundwater can transport such chemicals, it is important that the habitat is buffered on all sides by several feet (meters) of chemical-free land.

- The area must be free of predators or the habitat must be able to exclude them completely. Potential predators of uromastyx include foxes, raccoons, hawks, coyotes and domestic pets.

- The habitat must be installed in an area that is convenient to maintain, yet is located away from areas with high foot-traffic.

Outdoor cages vary in design, as most are custom built for the location. However, they all feature some type of walls, which create the enclosed area. Outdoor uromastyx habitats often resemble scaled-down versions of livestock pens. Several different materials can be used to construct the walls of the pen.

- Concrete blocks are sturdy, relatively inexpensive and easy to work with (although they are heavy). However, concrete blocks do not look very attractive, and without reinforcing them, they can topple. Further, it can be challenging to attach a roof to the top of the blocks.

- Corrugated plastic panels are lightweight, easy to work with and most animals cannot climb them. However, to be rigid enough, they must be attached to some sort of frame.

- Poured concrete walls are the best possible option, although constructing pens made of such walls is laborious and challenging. However, if you have the expertise, skill and finances to utilize poured concrete walls, they are unsurpassed in terms of utility, stability and aesthetics.

- Chain link fencing, chicken wire and similar materials are not appropriate for the pen walls. In addition to allowing some predators (such as rats) to enter the habitat, uromastyx may climb the material or become entangled in it, causing injury.

- Wood can be used to construct the walls, but it will need to be replaced as it rots or covered in an animal-safe sealant.

Regardless of the material used, the walls for a uromastyx pen must be at least 16 to 20 inches (40 to 50 centimeters) in height. In general, the higher the walls, the safer the lizards will be, but wall height will reduce the amount of sunlight that shines into the habitat when the sun is at a low angle. This may be a problem for keepers living at extreme latitudes.

One of the great benefits that outdoor cages provide in contrast to indoor cages is that it is usually easier to provide large accommodations for the uromastyx.

While it is possible to keep a uromastyx indoors in about 8 square feet of space (0.75 square meters), it is highly desirable to provide much more space than this. Strive for cages with 30 to 40 square feet (2.7 to 3.7 square meters) of space for up to three uromastyx.

On top of the cage, it is usually desirable to place some type of cover. If the walls are smooth and adequately tall -- at least 6 feet (3 meters) -- then most predators will be excluded. However, this does nothing to stop hawks, vultures, owls and other predator birds, from snacking on the lizards. Additionally, raccoons or opossums may climb into the cage from an overhanging tree or structure.

Be sure to allow the natural, unfiltered sunlight to bathe part of the pen, so glass, plastic and opaque materials are not good choices for the lid of an outdoor habitat.

While not appropriate for the cage walls, chain link fence, chicken wire and hardware cloth are good materials for the top of an outdoor habitat. They will require some type of frame to remain in place. The lid will have to be removable unless the cage is tall enough to permit you to walk into it from the side.

Another great benefit of outdoor habitats is that they allow a deep substrate. This is especially valuable for uromastyx, who often dig burrows in the wild. The challenge for the keeper is providing a suitable quantity and quality of substrate while preventing the captive from tunneling out of the cage or undermining cage props or walls.

The best substrates for uromastyx approximate those of their natural habitat. Usually, a mixture of one-part sand to one-part coconut fiber produces a light, well-drained mix that permits burrowing. Topsoil or naturally occurring clay may be used as well, but it must be able to retain water and hold its shape when your pet tries to create a burrow.

Ensure that the habitat's walls extend about 18 to 24 (45 to 60 cm) inches below ground level to reduce the chances that your uromastyx will dig under the wall and escape. Further protection can be had by attaching a 12-inch (25-centimeter) length of chicken wire or hardware cloth to the bottom of each wall panel. Place the chicken wire in the hole (which may need widening) so that it extends directly from the base of the wall to the inside of the pen. This way, if your uromastyx digs down past the bottom of the wall, it will run into the hardware cloth, thus blocking his attempts at tunneling to freedom.

Always be sure that outdoor habitats feature many different microclimates. Try to include flat areas that receive full morning sun, as well as places that provide deep shade to escape from the sun during the middle of the day.

Indoor Enclosures

Despite the appeal of outdoor caging, many people opt to keep their uromastyx indoors. Indoor maintenance is possible, but the endeavor is often more difficult to execute as the keeper must replicate the sun, and space constraints are often more severe indoors.

In "the old days," those inclined to keep reptiles had few choices with regard to caging. The two primary options were to build a custom cage from scratch or construct a lid to use with a fish aquarium.

By contrast, modern hobbyists have a variety of options from which to choose. In addition to building custom cages or adapting aquaria, dozens of different cage styles are available – each with different pros and cons.

Aquariums

Aquariums are popular choices for many pet reptiles and they are available at virtually every pet store in the country. However, they present several challenges for uromastyx maintenance and are not ideal for this purpose.

While many 10- and 20-gallon aquariums have footprints that are acceptable for housing very small uromastyx, few aquariums are manufactured in the appropriate layout for adults. While small aquariums have a large footprint relative to their volume, large aquariums have small footprints relative to their volume. This is because they are designed for fish rather than reptiles, who use their available space in different ways.

Also, aquariums are built so that the top of the enclosure serves as the opening, rather than the front. This can make it difficult to access the animal or clean the enclosure if the heat lamps and full-spectrum bulbs are resting on top of the cage.

One final, but important, drawback to aquariums is their weight. Large aquariums – particularly those loaded with substrate, rocks and perches -- are very heavy. Most will require two people to lift and move. Additionally, the glass construction makes aquariums very fragile enclosures, which can break very easily

Commercial Cages

Commercially produced reptile enclosures (such as those designed for snakes) are widely regarded as the best choice for uromastyx maintenance.

Most commercial cages are made of plastic or glass, and they feature doors on the front of the enclosure, rather than on the top. This means that they provide better access to the enclosure than aquariums do. Additionally, commercial reptile cages usually feature better footprint-to-volume ratios than aquariums do.

Commercial cages are usually sturdier than glass aquariums and lighter too. This makes them much easier to handle and move than aquariums.

Custom Built Cages

For keepers with access to tools and the desire and skill to use them, it is possible to construct homemade cages.

A number of materials are suitable for cage construction, and each has different pros and cons. Wood is commonly used but must be adequately sealed to avoid rotting, warping or absorbing offensive odors.

Plastic sheeting is a very good material, but few have the necessary skills, knowledge and tools necessary for cage construction. Additionally, some plastics may have extended off-gassing times.

Glass can be used, whether glued to itself or when used with a frame. Custom-built glass cages can be better than aquariums, as you can design them in dimensions that are appropriate for uromastyx. Additionally, they can be constructed in such a way that the door is on the front of the cage, rather than the top.

In all cases, the cages should be designed to contain the lizard safely, provide an adequate amount of floor space and allow the keeper suitable access.

Plastic Storage Containers

Plastic storage containers, such as those used for shoes, sweaters or food, can make sufficient enclosures for uromastyx.

While they are not particularly pretty, plastic storage boxes offer a number of advantages over other cage styles. This is especially true when housing small lizards.

For example, plastic storage boxes are much lighter than either aquariums or commercial cages, and they are less likely to break. Plastic storage containers are almost always much cheaper than cages or aquariums of similar size.

Usually, in order for plastic storage containers to serve as convenient housing, they must be tall enough to contain the lizards without the need for a lid. Obviously, this is not advisable in homes with pets or small children.

Plastic containers are rarely available in sizes appropriate for large uromastyx, but enterprising keepers may use cattle stock tanks or prefabricated pond liners instead.

Animals Per Enclosure

Often, keepers prefer keeping more than one animal in the same habitat. While this requires careful thought, planning and execution on the part of the keeper, it is possible in some cases. However, beginners often underestimate the increased workload that multiple animals generate.

Because uromastyx live in such an unusual habitat and are so uniquely adapted to it, few other species would thrive in similar conditions. Accordingly, they should not be housed with other species.

Many breeders and keepers house uromastyx in small groups. While generally acceptable, the process requires more work and forethought than is commonly used. Rather than simply acquiring a group of uromastyx and placing them together in a cage, it is important that you consider the following issues:

- The uromastyx must have all passed through individual quarantine periods and be free of pathogens before they are housed together. While quarantine cages need not be as large as the long-term home for the animals, they must still be large enough to allow the animals to thermoregulate and get enough exercise.

- Many uromastyx – particularly males -- will fight over burrows and territory, which can lead to serious injuries. Accordingly, the best strategy is to keep one male with several females.

- While you need not double the size of the enclosure for every uromastyx you add to the colony, the total area must be large enough for all of the animals to enjoy their own burrow and have enough room to exercise.

- Not all uromastyx will cohabitate amicably. This phenomenon is not limited to males; females will occasionally exhibit antagonistic behaviors towards other females.

- Always observe new additions carefully for several weeks to ensure they are cohabitating well with the others in the cage. While the uromastyx may all get along initially, the social dynamics of the colony may change over time.

Chapter 7: Establishing the Thermal Environment

Providing the proper thermal environment is one of the most important aspects of reptile husbandry. As ectothermic ("cold-blooded") animals, uromastyx rely on the surrounding temperatures to regulate the rate at which their metabolism operates.

Providing a proper thermal environment can mean the difference between a healthy, thriving uromastyx and one who spends a great deal of time at the veterinarian's office, battling infections and illness.

While individuals may demonstrate slightly different preferences, and different species have slightly different preferences, most active uromastyx prefer ambient temperatures in the high-80s Fahrenheit (about 30 degrees Celsius). Inactive (sleeping) uromastyx prefer temperatures in the low 70s Fahrenheit (21 to 23 degrees Celsius).

However, while these are appropriate air temperatures for uromastyx, they will also require a very warm basking spot during the day, with a temperature of about 120 to 130 degrees Fahrenheit (48 to 54 degrees Celsius).

Providing your uromastyx with a suitable thermal environment requires the correct approach, the correct heating equipment and the tools necessary for monitoring the thermal environment.

Size-Related Heating Concerns

Before examining the best way to establish a proper thermal environment, it is important to understand that your lizard's body size influences the way in which he heats up and cools off.

Because volume increases more quickly than surface area does with increasing body size, small individuals experience more rapid temperature fluctuations than larger individuals do.

Accordingly, it is imperative to protect small individuals from temperature extremes. Conversely, larger uromastyx are more tolerant of temperature extremes than smaller individuals are (though they should still be protected from temperature extremes).

Thermal Gradients

In the wild, uromastyx move between different microhabitats so that they can maintain ideal body temperature as much as possible.

The best way to do this is by clustering the heating devices at one end of the habitat, thereby creating a basking spot (the warmest spot in the enclosure).

The temperatures will slowly drop with increasing distance from the basking spot, which creates a *gradient* of temperatures. Barriers, such as branches and vegetation, also help to create shaded patches, which provide additional thermal options.

This mimics the way temperatures vary from one small place to the next in your pet's natural habitat. For example, a wild uromastyx may move under some vegetation too cool off at midday, or move onto a sun-bathed rock to warm up in the morning.

By establishing a gradient in the enclosure, your captive uromastyx will be able to access a range of different temperatures, which will allow him to manage his body temperature just as his wild counterparts do.

Adjust the heating device until the surface temperatures at the basking spot are between 120 and 130 degrees Fahrenheit (48 to 54 degrees Celsius). Provide a slightly cooler basking spot for immature individuals, with maximum temperatures of about 115 degrees Fahrenheit (46 degrees Celsius).

Because there is no heat source at the other end of the cage, the ambient temperature will gradually fall as your uromastyx moves away from the heat source. Ideally, the cool end of the cage should be in the low 70s Fahrenheit (22 degrees Celsius).

The need to establish a thermal gradient is one of the most compelling reasons to use a roomy cage. In general, the larger the cage, the easier it is to establish a suitable thermal gradient.

Heating Equipment

There are a variety of different heating devices you can use to keep your uromastyx' habitat within the appropriate temperature range.

Be sure to consider your choice carefully, and select the best type of heating device for you and your lizard.

Heat Lamps

Heat lamps are usually the best choice for supplying heat to your lizard's habitat. Heat lamps consist of a reflector dome and an incandescent bulb. The light bulb produces heat (in addition to light) and the metal reflector dome directs the heat to a spot inside the cage.

You will need to clamp the lamp to a stable anchor or part of the cage's frame. Always be sure that the lamp is securely attached and will not be dislodged by vibration, children or pets.

Because fire safety is always a concern, and many keepers use high-wattage light bulbs, opt for heavy-duty reflector domes with ceramic bases, rather than economy units with plastic bases. The price difference is negligible, given the stakes.

One of the greatest benefits of using heat lamps to maintain the temperature of your pet's habitat is the flexibility they offer. While you can adjust the amount of heat provided by heat tapes and other devices with a rheostat or thermostat, you can adjust the enclosure temperature provided by heat lamps in two ways:

- Changing the Bulb Wattage

The simplest way to adjust the temperature of your pet's cage is by changing the wattage of the bulb you are using.

For example, if a 40-watt light bulb is not raising the temperature of the basking spot high enough, you may try a 60-watt bulb. Alternatively, if a 100-watt light bulb is elevating the cage temperatures higher than are appropriate, switching to a 60-watt bulb may help.

- Adjusting the Distance between the Heat Lamp and the Basking Spot

The closer the heat lamp is to the cage, the warmer the cage will be. If the habitat is too warm, you can move the light farther from the enclosure, which should lower the basking spot temperatures slightly.

However, the farther away you move the lamp, the larger the basking spot becomes. It is important to be careful that you do not move it too far away, which will reduce the effectiveness of the thermal gradient by heating the enclosure too uniformly. In very large cages, this may not compromise the thermal gradient very much, but in a small cage, it may eliminate the "cool side" of the habitat.

In other words, if your heat lamp creates a basking spot that is roughly 1-foot in diameter when it is 1 inch away from the screen, it will produce a slightly cooler, but larger basking spot when moved back another 6 inches or so.

Ceramic Heat Emitters

Ceramic heat emitters are small inserts that function similarly to light bulbs, except that they do not produce any visible light – they only produce heat.

Ceramic heat emitters are used in reflector-dome fixtures, just as heat lamps are. The benefits of such devices are numerous:

- They typically last much longer than light bulbs do

- They are suitable for use with thermostats

- They allow for the creation of overhead basking spots, as lights do

- They can be used day or night

However, the devices do have three primary drawbacks:

- They are very hot when in operation

- They are much more expensive than light bulbs

- You cannot tell by looking if they are hot or cool. This can be a safety hazard – touching a ceramic heat emitter while it is hot is likely to cause serious burns.

Radiant Heat Panels

Quality radiant heat panels are a great choice for heating most reptile habitats, including those containing uromastyx. Radiant heat panels are essentially heat pads that stick to the roof of the habitat. They usually feature rugged, plastic or metal casings and internal reflectors to direct the infrared heat back into the cage.

Radiant heat panels have a number of benefits over traditional heat lamps and under tank heat pads:

- They do not produce visible light, which means they are useful for both diurnal and nocturnal heat production. They can be used in conjunction with fluorescent light fixtures during the day, and remain on at night once the lights go off.

- They are inherently flexible. Unlike many devices that do not work well with pulse-proportional thermostats, most radiant heat panels work well with on-off and pulse-proportional thermostats.

The only real drawback to radiant heat panels is their cost: radiant heat panels often cost about two to three times the price of light- or heat pad-oriented systems. However, many radiant heat panels outlast light bulbs and heat pads, a fact that offsets their high initial cost over the long term.

Heat Pads

Heat pads are an attractive option for many new keepers, but they are not without drawbacks.

- Heat pads have a high risk of causing contact burns.

- If they malfunction, they can damage the cage as well as the surface on which they are placed.

- They are more likely to cause a fire than heat lamps or radiant heat panels are.

However, if installed properly (which includes allowing fresh air to flow over the exposed side of the heat pad) and used in conjunction with a thermostat, they can be reasonably safe. With heat pads, it behooves the keeper to purchase premium products, despite the small increase in price.

Heat Tape
Heat tape is somewhat akin to a "stripped down" heat pad. In fact, most heat pads are simply pieces of heat tape that have already been connected and sealed inside a plastic envelope.

Heat tape is primarily used to heat large numbers of cages simultaneously. It is generally inappropriate for novices and requires the keeper to make electrical connections. Additionally, a thermostat is always required when using heat tape.

Historically, heat tape was used to keep water pipes from freezing – not to heat reptile cages. While some commercial heat tapes have been designed specifically for reptiles, many have not. Accordingly, it may be illegal, not to mention dangerous, to use heat tapes for purposes other than for which they are designed.

Heat Cables
Heat cables are similar to heat tape, in that they heat a long strip of the cage, but they are much more flexible and easy to use. Many heat cables are suitable to use inside the cage, while others are designed for use outside the habitat.

Always be sure to purchase heat cables that are designed to be used in reptile cages. Those sold at hardware stores are not appropriate for use in a cage.

Heat cables must be used in conjunction with a thermostat, or, at the very least, a rheostat.

Nocturnal Temperatures

Because uromastyx easily tolerate temperatures in the low-70s Fahrenheit (21 to 22 degrees Celsius) at night, most keepers can allow their pet's habitat to fall to ambient room temperature at night.

Because it is important to avoid using lights on your lizard's habitat at night, those living in homes with lower nighttime temperatures will need to employ additional heat sources. Most such keepers accomplish this through the use of ceramic heat emitters.

Thermometers

It is important to monitor the cage temperatures very carefully to ensure your pet stays healthy. Just as a water test kit is an aquarist's best friend, quality thermometers are some of the most important husbandry tools for reptile keepers.

Ambient and Surface Temperatures

Two different types of temperature are relevant for pet uromastyx: ambient temperatures and surface temperatures.

The ambient temperature in your animal's enclosure is the air temperature; the surface temperatures are the temperatures of the objects in the cage. Both are important to monitor, as they can differ widely.

Measure the cage's ambient temperatures with a digital thermometer. An indoor-outdoor model will feature a probe that allows you to measure the temperature at both ends of the thermal gradient at once. For example, you may position the thermometer at the cool side of the cage, but attach the remote probe to a branch near the basking spot.

Because standard digital thermometers do not measure surface temperatures well, use a non-contact, infrared thermometer for such measurements. These devices will allow you to measure surface temperatures accurately from a short distance away.

Thermostats and Rheostats

Some heating devices, such as heat lamps, are designed to operate at full capacity for the entire time that they are turned on. Such devices should not be used with thermostats – instead, care should be taken to calibrate the proper temperature by tweaking the bulb wattage.

Other devices, such as heat pads, heat tape and radiant heat panels are designed to be used with a regulating device, such as a thermostat or rheostat, which maintains the proper temperature

Rheostats

Rheostats are similar to light-dimmer switches, and they allow you to reduce the output of a heating device. In this way, you can dial in the proper temperature for the habitat.

The drawback to rheostats is that they only regulate the amount of power going to the device – they do not monitor the cage temperature or adjust the power flow automatically. In practice, even with the same level of power entering the device, the amount of heat generated by most heat sources will vary over the course of the day.

If you set the rheostat so that it keeps the cage at the right temperature in the morning, it may become too hot by the middle of the day. Conversely, setting the proper temperature during the middle of the day may leave the morning temperatures too cool.

Care must be taken to ensure that the rheostat controller is not inadvertently bumped or jostled, causing the temperature to rise or fall outside of healthy parameters.

Thermostats

Thermostats are similar to rheostats, except that they also feature a temperature probe that monitors the temperature in the cage (or under the basking source). This allows the thermostat to adjust the power going to the device as necessary to maintain a predetermined temperature.

For example, if you place the temperature probe under a basking spot powered by a radiant heat panel, the thermostat will keep the temperature relatively constant at the basking site.

There are two different types of thermostats:

- On-Off Thermostats

On-Off Thermostats work by cutting the power to the device when the probe's temperature reaches a given temperature. For example, if the thermostat were set to 85 degrees Fahrenheit (29 degrees Celsius), the heating device would turn off whenever the temperature exceeds this threshold. When the temperature falls below 85, the thermostat restores power to the unit, and the heater begins functioning again. This cycle will continue to repeat, thus maintaining the temperature within a relatively small range.

Be aware that on-off thermostats have a "lag" factor, meaning that they do not turn off when the temperature reaches a given temperature. They turn off when the temperature is a few degrees above that temperature, and then turn back on when the temperate is a little below the set point. Because of this, it is important to avoid setting the temperature at the limits of your pet's acceptable range. Some premium models have an adjustable amount of threshold for this factor, which is helpful.

- Pulse Proportional Thermostats

Pulse proportional thermostats work by constantly sending pulses of electricity to the heater. By varying the rate of pulses, the amount of energy reaching the heating devices varies. A small computer inside the thermostat adjusts this rate to match the set-point temperature as measured by the probe. Accordingly, pulse proportional thermostats maintain much more consistent temperatures than on-off thermostats do.

Lights should not be used with thermostats, as the constant flickering may stress your pet. Conversely, heat pads, heat tape, radiant heat panels and ceramic heat emitters should always be used with either a rheostat or, preferably, a thermostat to avoid overheating your pet.

Thermostat Failure

If used for long enough, all thermostats eventually fail. The question is will yours fail today or twenty years from now. While some thermostats fail in the "off" position, a thermostat that fails in the "on" position may overheat your uromastyx. Unfortunately, tales of entire collections being lost to a faulty thermostat are too common.

Accordingly, it behooves the keeper to acquire high-quality thermostats. Some keepers use two thermostats, connected in a series arrangement. By setting the second thermostat (the "backup thermostat") a few degrees higher than the setting used on the "primary thermostat," you safeguard yourself against the failure of either unit.

In such a scenario, the backup thermostat allows the full power coming to it to travel through to the heating device, as the temperature never reaches its higher set-point temperature.

However, if the first unit fails in the "on" position, the second thermostat will keep the temperatures from rising too high. The temperature will rise a few degrees in accordance with the higher set-point temperature, but it will not get hot enough to harm your pets.

If the backup thermostat fails in the "on" position, the first thermostat retains control. If either fails in the "off" position, the temperature will fall until you rectify the situation, but a brief exposure to relatively cool temperatures is unlikely to be fatal.

Chapter 8: Lighting the Enclosure

Given the amount of time they spend hanging out in the sun, it should come as no surprise that uromastyx have evolved to depend upon it.

It is always preferable to afford captive uromastyx access to unfiltered sunlight, but this is not always possible. In these cases, it is necessary to provide your uromastyx with high-quality lighting, which can partially satisfy their need for real sunlight.

Uromastyx deprived of appropriate lighting may become seriously ill. Learning how to provide the proper lighting for reptiles is sometimes an arduous task for beginners, but it is very important to the long-term health of your pet that you do. To understand the type of light your lizard needs, you must first understand a little bit about light.

The Electromagnetic Spectrum

Light is a type of energy that physicists call electromagnetic radiation; it travels in waves. These waves may differ in amplitude, which correlates to the vertical distance between consecutive wave crests and troughs, frequency, which correlates with the number of crests per unit of time, and wavelength.

Wavelength is the distance from one crest to the next or one trough to the next. Wavelength and frequency are inversely proportional, meaning that as the wavelength increases, the frequency decreases. It is more common for reptile keepers to discuss wavelengths rather than frequencies.

The sun produces energy (light) with a very wide range of constituent wavelengths. Some of these wavelengths fall within a range called the visible spectrum; humans can detect these rays with their eyes. Such waves have wavelengths between about 390 and 700 nanometers. Rays with wavelengths longer or shorter than these limits are broken into their own groups and given different names.

Those rays with around 390-nanometer wavelengths or less are called ultraviolet rays or UV rays. UV rays are broken down into three different categories, just as the different colors correspond to different wavelengths of visible light. UVA rays have wavelengths between 315 to 400 nanometers, while UVB rays have wavelengths between 280 and 315 nanometers while UVC rays have wavelengths between 100 and 280 nanometers.

Rays with wavelengths of less than 280 nanometers are called x-rays and gamma rays. At the other end of the spectrum, infrared rays have wavelengths longer than 700 nanometers; microwaves and radio waves are even longer.

UVA rays are important for food recognition, appetite, activity and eliciting natural behaviors. UVB rays are necessary for many reptiles to produce vitamin D3. Without this vitamin, reptiles cannot properly metabolize their calcium.

Light Color

The light that comes from the sun and light bulbs is composed of a combination of wavelengths, which create the blended white light that you perceive. This combination of wavelengths varies slightly from one light source to the next.

The sun produces very balanced white light, while "economy" incandescent bulbs produce relatively fewer blue rays and yields a yellow-looking light. High-quality bulbs designed for reptiles often produce very balanced, white light. The degree to which light causes objects to look as they would under sunlight is called the Color Rendering Index, or CRI. Sunlight has a CRI of 100, while quality bulbs have CRIs of 80 to 90; by contrast, a typical incandescent bulb has a CRI of 40 to 50

Light Brightness

Another important characteristic of light that relates to uromastyx is luminosity or the brightness of light. Measured in units called Lux, luminosity is an important consideration for your lighting system. While you cannot possibly replicate the intensity of the sun's light, it is desirable in most circumstances to ensure the habitat is lit as well as is reasonably possible.

For example, in the tropics, the sunlight intensity averages around 100,000 Lux at midday; by comparison, the lights in a typical family living room only produce about 50 Lux.

Without bright lighting, many reptiles become lethargic, depressed or exhibit hibernating behaviors. Dim lighting may inhibit feeding and cause lizards to become stressed and ill.

Your Lizard's Lighting Needs

To reiterate, uromastyx (and most other lizards) require:

- Light that is comprised of visible light, as well as UVA and UVB wavelengths
- Light with a high color-rendering index
- Light of the sufficiently strong intensity

Now that you know what your lizard requires, you can go about designing the lighting system for his habitat. Ultraviolet radiation is the most difficult component of proper lighting to provide, so it makes sense to begin by examining the types of bulbs that produce UV radiation.

The only commercially produced bulbs that produce significant amounts of UVA and UVB and suitable for a uromastyx habitat are linear fluorescent light bulbs, compact fluorescent light bulbs and mercury vapor bulbs.

Neither type of fluorescent bulb produces significant amounts of heat, but mercury vapor bulbs produce a lot of heat and serve a dual function. In many cases, keepers elect to use both types of lights – a mercury vapor bulb for a warm basking site with high levels of UV radiation and fluorescent bulbs to light the rest of the cage without raising the temperature. You can also use fluorescent bulbs to provide the requisite UV radiation and use a regular incandescent bulb to generate the basking spot.

Fluorescent bulbs have a much longer history of use than mercury vapor bulbs, which makes some keepers more comfortable using them. However, many models only produce moderate amounts of UVB radiation. While some mercury vapor bulbs produce significant quantities of UVB, some question the wisdom of producing more UV radiation than the animal receives in the wild. Additionally, mercury vapor bulbs are much too powerful to use in small habitats, and they are more expensive initially.

Most fluorescent bulbs must be placed within 12 inches of the basking surface, while some mercury vapor bulbs should be placed farther away from the basking surface – be sure to read the manufacturer's instructions before use. Be sure that the bulbs you purchase specifically state the amount of UVB radiation they produce; this figure is expressed as a percentage, for example, 7% UVB. Most UVB-producing bulbs require replacement every six to 12 months – whether or not they have stopped producing light.

However, ultraviolet radiation is only one of the characteristics that lizard keepers must consider. The light bulbs used must also produce a sunlight-like spectrum. Fortunately, most high-quality light bulbs that produce significant amounts of UVA and UVB radiation also feature a high color-rendering index. The higher the CRI, the better, but any bulbs with a CRI of 90 or above will work well. If you are having trouble deciding between two otherwise evenly matched bulbs, select the one with the higher CRI value.

Brightness is the final, and easiest, consideration for the keeper to address. While no one yet knows what the ideal luminosity for a uromastyx' cage, it makes sense to ensure that at least part of the cage features very bright lighting. However, you should always offer a shaded retreat within the enclosure into which your lizard can avoid the light if he desires.

Connect the lights to an electric timer to keep the length of the day and night consistent. Some breeders manipulate their captive's photoperiod over the course of the year to prime the animals for breeding, but pet uromastyx thrive with 12 hours of daylight and 12 hours of darkness all year long.

Chapter 9: Substrate and Furniture

Substrate choice is an important consideration for your uromastyx' enclosure, as they occasionally burrow into the substrate in the wild to escape oppressive temperatures or avoid detection by predators while they are sleeping.

Accordingly, the substrate must yield easily enough that the lizard can dig into it, yet it must retain its structural integrity enough to permit the construction of stable tunnels.

Many different hobbyists and breeders swear by a given recipe for making the perfect uromastyx substrate. As long as such recipes contain no toxic or harmful types of soil, do not produce excess dust and allow the uromastyx to burrow, they should all be acceptable.

Most such recipes feature varying amounts of play sand and either coconut fiber or organic topsoil. The sand helps to prevent the substrate from holding too much moisture and ensures adequate drainage, while the coconut fiber or soil has enough moisture and the proper type of structure, to maintain burrows.

It is a good idea to sift any substrates before placing them in your uromastyx' pen to prevent including harmful items that may have made their way into the substrate, such as nails, sharp sticks or trash.

Cage Furniture

To complete your uromastyx habitat, you must provide him with visual barriers and places to hide. You may also want to add things for aesthetic value and your own enjoyment.

Cork Bark

The outer bark of the cork oak tree (*Quercus suber*), cork bark is available in both tubes and flat slabs. Tubes work best for uromastyx maintenance, although you can come up with creative ways to use flat pieces in many cases.

The primary downsides to cork bark relate to its price (it is often rather expensive) and its tendency to collect debris in the cracks on its surface, which makes cleaning difficult.

Cardboard and Other Disposable Hides

Cardboard tubes, boxes or sheets also make excellent hiding spaces, as do sections of foam egg crate. These materials are lightweight, very low cost and easy to replace once soiled. Try to arrange these items in ways that mimic some of the hiding places uromastyx would use in the wild.

Plastic Containers

You can make functional – if not pretty – hides with inverted plastic containers that have a hole cut into the side to provide a door.

Plastic containers are an affordable choice, and they are quite easy to keep clean. However, it is important to pick containers that will provide a tight space in which your uromastyx can hide, rather than a gigantic box, which won't provide the security your uromastyx desires. It is also wise to use an opaque box, rather than a translucent one, for similar, security-related reasons.

Plants

Live plants may require more work and effort on the part of the keeper, but they offer a place for your pet to slip out of sight, and they look nice too.

Always wash all plants before placing them in the enclosure to help remove any pesticide residues. It is also wise to discard the potting soil used for the plant and replace it with fresh soil, which you know contains no pesticides, perlite or fertilizer.

While you can plant cage plants directly in soil substrates, this complicates maintenance and makes it difficult to replace the substrate regularly. Accordingly, it is generally preferable to keep the plant in some type of container. Be sure to use a catch tray under the pot, so that water draining from the container does not flow into the cage.

You must use care to select a species that will thrive in your uromastyx' enclosure. This essentially means selecting plants that will thrive in an arid climate. They must also be able to thrive in relatively low-light conditions if you are keeping your pets indoors.

Be aware that your uromastyx may nibble on any plants included in the enclosure, so be sure to stick with non-toxic species.

Chapter 10: Maintaining the Captive Habitat

Now that you have acquired your uromastyx and set up the enclosure, you must develop a protocol for maintaining his habitat. While uromastyx habitats require major maintenance every month or so, they only require minor daily maintenance.

In addition to designing a husbandry protocol, you must embrace a record-keeping system to track your uromastyx' growth and health.

Cleaning and Maintenance Procedures

Once you have decided on the proper enclosure for your pet, you must keep your uromastyx fed, hydrated and ensure that the habitat stays in proper working order to keep your captive healthy and comfortable.

Some tasks must be completed each day, while others are should be performed weekly, monthly or annually.

Daily

- Monitor the ambient and surface temperatures of the habitat.

- Spot clean the cage to remove any loose insects, feces, urates or pieces of shed skin.

- Ensure that the lights, latches and other moving parts are in working order.

- Verify that your uromastyx is acting normally and appears healthy. You do not necessarily need to handle him to do so.

- Feed your uromastyx a plate of fresh vegetables (note that some keepers only feed their captives three or four times per week).

Weekly
- Change sheet-like substrates (newspaper, paper towels, etc.).

- Clean the inside surfaces of the enclosure.

- Inspect your uromastyx closely for any signs of injury, parasites or illness.

- Wash and sterilize all food dishes.

Monthly
- Break down the cage completely, remove and discard particulate substrates.

- Sterilize drip containers and similar equipment in a mild bleach solution.

- Measure and weigh your uromastyx.

- Photograph your pet (recommended, but not imperative).

- Prune any plants as necessary.

Annually
- Replace the batteries in your thermometers and any other devices that use them.

- Replace UVB lights (some require replacement every six months)

Cleaning your uromastyx' cage and furniture is relatively simple. Regardless of the way it became soiled, the basic process remains the same:

1. Rinse the object
2. Using a scrub brush or sponge and soapy water, remove any organic debris from the object.
3. Rinse the object thoroughly.
4. Disinfect the object.

5. Re-rinse the object.
6. Dry the object.

Chemicals & Tools

A variety of chemicals and tools are necessary for reptile care. Save yourself some time by purchasing dedicated cleaning products and keeping them in the same place that you keep your tools.

Spray Bottles

Misting your uromastyx and his habitat with fresh water is one of the best ways to provide him with drinking water. You can do this with a small, handheld misting bottle or a larger, pressurized unit (such as those used to spray herbicides). Automated units are available, but they are rarely cost-effective unless you are caring for a large colony of animals.

Small Brooms

Small brooms are great for sweeping up small messes and bits of substrate. It is usually helpful to select one that features angled bristles, as they'll allow you to better reach the nooks and crannies of your pet's cage and the surrounding area.

Ideally, the broom should come with its own dustpan to collect debris, but there are plenty of workarounds for those that don't come with their own.

Scrub Brushes or Sponges

It helps to have a few different types of scrub brushes and sponges on hand for scrubbing and cleaning different items. Use the least abrasive sponge or brush suitable for the task to prevent wearing out cage items prematurely. Do not use abrasive materials on glass or acrylic surfaces. Steel-bristled brushes work well for scrubbing coarse, wooden items, such as branches.

Spatulas and Putty Knives
Spatulas, putty knives and similar tools are often helpful for cleaning reptile cages. For example, urates (which are not soluble in anything short of hot lava) often become stuck on cage walls or furniture. Instead of trying to dissolve them with harsh chemicals, just scrape them away with a sturdy plastic putty knife.

Small Vacuums
Small, handheld vacuums are very helpful for sucking up the dust left behind from substrates. They are also helpful for cleaning the cracks and crevices around the cage doors. A shop vacuum, with suitable hoses and attachments, can also be helpful if you have enough room to store it.

Soap
Use a gentle, non-scented dish soap. Antibacterial soap is preferred, but not necessary. Most people use far more soap than is necessary -- a few drops mixed with a quantity of water is usually sufficient to help remove surface pollutants.

Bleach
Bleach (diluted to one-half cup per gallon of water) makes an excellent disinfectant. Be careful not to spill any on clothing, carpets or furniture, as it is likely to discolor the objects.

Always be sure to rinse objects thoroughly after using bleach and be sure that you cannot detect any residual odor. Bleach does not work as a disinfectant when in contact with organic substances; accordingly, items must be cleaned before you can disinfect them.

Veterinarian Approved Disinfectant
Many commercial products are available that are designed to be safe for their pets. Consult with your veterinarian about

the best product for your situation, its method of use and its proper dilution.

Avoid Phenols
Always avoid cleaners that contain phenols, as they are extremely toxic to some reptiles. In general, do not use household cleaning products to avoid exposing your pet to toxic chemicals.

Keeping Records
It is important to keep records regarding your pet's health, growth and feeding, as well as any other important details. In the past, reptile keepers would do so on small index cards or in a notebook. In the modern world, technological solutions may be easier.

You can record as much information about your pet as you like, and the more information to you record, the better. But minimally, you should record the following:

Pedigree and Origin Information
Be sure to record the source of your uromastyx, the date on which you acquired him and any other data that is available. Breeders will often provide customers with information regarding the sire, dam, date of birth, weights and feeding records, but other sources will rarely offer comparable data.

Feeding Information
Record the date of each feeding, as well as the type of food item(s) offered. It is also helpful to record any preferences you may observe or any meals that are refused.

It is also wise to record the times you supplement the food with calcium or vitamin powders unless you employ a standard weekly protocol.

Weights and Length

Because you look at your pet frequently, it is difficult to appreciate how quickly he is (or isn't) growing. Accordingly, it is important to track his size diligently.

Weigh your uromastyx with a high-quality digital scale. It is often easiest to use a dedicated "weighing container" with a known weight to measure your pet. Simply subtract the weight of the container to obtain the weight of your uromastyx.

You can measure your uromastyx' length as well, but it is not as important as his weight.

Maintenance Information

Record all of the noteworthy events associated with your pet's care. While it is not necessary to note that you misted the cage every other day, it is appropriate to record the dates on which you changed the substrate or sterilized the cage.

North African uromastyx (Uromastyx acanithura)

Whenever you purchase new equipment, supplies or caging, note the date and source. This not only helps to remind you when you purchased the items, but it may help you track down a source for the items in the future, if necessary.

Breeding Information

If you intend to breed your uromastyx, you should record all details associated with pre-breeding conditioning, cycling, introductions, matings, color changes, copulations and egg deposition.

Record all pertinent information about any resulting clutches as well, including the number of viable eggs, as well as the number of unhatched and unfertilized eggs.

Additionally, if you keep several uromastyx together in the same enclosure, you'll want to be careful to document the details of egg deposition, so you can be sure you know the correct parentage of each egg.

Record Keeping Samples

The following are two different examples of suitable recording systems.

The first example is reminiscent of the style employed by many with large collections. Because such keepers often have numerous animals, the notes are very simple.

The second example demonstrates a simple approach that is employed by many with small collections (or a single pet): keeping notes on paper. Such notes could be taken in a notebook or journal, or you could type directly into a word processor. It does not matter *how* you keep records, just that you *do* keep records.

Number:	44522	Genus: Species:	Uromastyx geyri	Gender: DOB:	Male 3/20/1 4	CAR D #2
6.30.15 Greens and seed	7.03.15 Crickets	7.07.15 Greens and seed	7.11.15 Greens and seed	7.15.15 Greens and seed		
7.01.15 Grass and flowers	7.05.15 Greens and fruit	7.08.15 Greens and fruit	7.12.15 Greens and fruit	7.16.15 Sterilized Cage		
7.02.15 Greens and seed	7.06.15 Grass and seed	7.10.15 Weight: 300 grams	7.14.15 Grass and flowers			

Date	Notes
4-26-13	Acquired "Uri" the Saharan Uromastyx from a lizard breeder named Mark at the in-town reptile expo. Mark explained that Uri's scientific name is Uromastyx geyri – that should be easy to remember! He cost $250. Mark said he purchased the lizard in March, but he does not know the exact date.
4-27-13	Uri spent the night in the container I bought him in. I purchased a small plastic storage box cage, a heat lamp and a thermometer at the hardware store, and I ordered a non-contact thermometer and full-spectrum light online. I added a small cardboard box so he had somewhere to hide.
4-28-13	Uri eagerly drank when I put a water dish in front of him. He was also hungry! He ate a

	huge plate of veggies in about 5 minutes.
4-29-13	*I fed Uri another plate of greens today. He ate them as quickly as he ate the first.*
4-30-13	*Robert ate another big plate of food today. I also gave him three crickets, which he gobbled up quickly.*

Chapter 11: Feeding Uromastyx

Feeding your uromastyx a healthy diet is one of the most important aspects of his care. This not only means providing your pet with suitable food items but providing them in the proper way, in the appropriate amounts and on a proper schedule.

Different types of foods for your uromastyx are detailed below. In general, you want to provide your uromastyx with a variety of leafy greens and vegetables, with a small amount of fruits, seed and insects mixed in from time to time.

Vegetables

Vegetables, particularly leafy green vegetables, should form the bulk of your uromastyx' diet. Just be sure to cut all large foods into bite-size pieces for your lizard.

- Endive

- Kale

- Escarole

- Radicchio

- Squash (sparingly)

- Zucchini (sparingly)

- Cucumber (sparingly)

- Parsley

- Collard greens

- Turnip greens

- Radish greens

- Carrot greens

- Cactus pads (thorns removed)

- Banana leaves

- Dill weed

- Lambs lettuce

- Arugula

- Cress

- Japanese radish greens

- Grape leaves

Leaves, Weeds and Flowers

Leaves, weeds, flowers and grasses can also be incorporated into your uromastyx' diet. Not all individuals will take these items, but they are healthy food sources.

- Mulberry leaves

- Petunia leaves and flowers

- Dandelion leaves and flowers

- Hibiscus leaves and flowers

- Rose leaves and flowers

- Clover leaves and flowers

- Common sorrel

- Basil

- Prickly pear (with spines removed)

- Blackberry leaves and flowers (remove thorns)

- Squash blossoms

- Alfalfa hay

- Timothy hay

- Bermuda grasses

- Fescue grasses

- Ryegrasses

- Couch grass

- Buffalo grass

- Kikuyu grass

- Blue Grama grass

- Dallas grass

- Wintergrass

- Bluegrass

- Wheatgrass

- Crabgrass

- Tall oat grass

- Orchard grass

- Raspberry leaves and flowers (remove thorns)

Fruits

Fruits should only make up a small part of your uromastyx' diet – perhaps 5% to 10% at most.

- Apples (remove cores and seeds)

- Pears

- Blackberries

- Raspberries

- Honeydew Melon

- Cantaloupe

- Mango

- Figs

- Persimmons

Preparing Food for Your Uromastyx

While a little dirt is unlikely to sicken your lizard, it makes sense to keep their food as clean as possible. Bacteria, fungi and parasites likely litter the ground of your pet's enclosure, so use a clean food dish or flat rock for your pet's supplemental meals.

Some keepers prepare "feeding trays" for their pets, which help to keep your pet from eating off the ground. To do so, fill several small, shallow trays with sterilized, organic potting soil. Then plant edible grass and plant seeds in the soil; after sprouting, place the tray in with your uromastyx, who can then feed on the tender, young plants. You will need to make several such trays and rotate them regularly if this is to be an important food source.

Feeding Frequency

The proper feeding frequency for your uromastyx depends on his size, species and age. Generally speaking, uromastyx should be fed four to seven times per week; the younger the lizard, the more often it should be fed.

As long as your uromastyx is healthy, gets plenty of exercise, has access to suitable temperatures and is provided with a wide variety of food items, you do not have to worry about over-feeding him during the first few years of life. However, mature animals – or those living in small cages – may become overweight if fed too frequently.

Ultimately, you must adjust your uromastyx' diet by monitoring his weight regularly. Young uromastyx should exhibit steady, moderate growth rates, while mature animals should maintain a relatively consistent body weight.

If your uromastyx fails to grow or begins losing weight, you must increase the frequency of his feedings. Conversely, those that gain excessive weight should be placed on restrictive diets. Consult with your veterinarian before altering your feeding schedule drastically.

Vitamin and Mineral Supplements

Many keepers add commercially produced vitamin and mineral supplements to their pet's food on a regular basis. In theory, these supplements help to correct dietary deficiencies and ensure that captive uromastyx get a balanced diet. In practice, things are not this simple.

While some vitamins and minerals are unlikely to build up to toxic levels, others may very well cause problems if provided in excess. This means that you cannot simply apply supplements to every meal – you must decide upon a sensible supplementation schedule.

Because the age, sex and health of your pet all influence the amount of vitamins and minerals your pet requires, and each individual product has a unique composition, it is wise to consult your veterinarian before deciding upon a supplementation schedule.

However, most keepers provide vitamin supplementation once each week, and calcium supplementation several times per week.

Despite the best efforts of uromastyx keepers to feed their pets a nutritious, well-balanced diet, it is a very hard task to accomplish. To help offset potential deficiencies, many uromastyx keepers supplement the diet of their lizard with extra minerals and vitamins.

Usually, such supplements come in powder or liquid form, and they are designed to be mixed in with a uromastyx' food or given orally. For obvious reasons, it is easier to mix supplements into your uromastyx' food, rather than try to coax him to open his mouth.

Most keepers use two different types of supplements: a multivitamin and a calcium powder. Sometimes, calcium powders are also fortified with vitamin D3 to ensure that the uromastyx can properly metabolize the calcium. Vitamins and calcium powder are best kept separate from each other to allow for differential doses.

The proper dosages of vitamins and calcium are poorly understood. If a uromastyx receives too much supplementation of either vitamins or calcium it can lead to serious health problems. To be safe, discuss your uromastyx' needs with your veterinarian to arrive at a safe dosage schedule. Although hypercalcemia (too much calcium in the bloodstream) is much rarer than hypocalcemia (too little calcium in the bloodstream), it is a possibility worth considering when devising a calcium supplementation schedule. While hypocalcemia causes a number of potential health problems, hypercalcemia can cause serious health problems as well, including renal failure.

Generally speaking, most uromastyx keepers provide vitamin supplements once per week. Calcium supplementation varies based on the age and gender of your uromastyx. Young, quickly growing uromastyx and reproductively active females require more calcium than adult males do.

If your uromastyx is housed outside, it is unlikely that he is deficient in vitamin D3, so opt for a calcium powder without it. By contrast, even though indoor uromastyx should be provided with UVB lighting to help them produce their own vitamin D3, they likely do not produce enough to metabolize all of their calcium.

Chapter 12: Providing Water to Your Uromastyx

Uromastyx have adapted to life in arid regions, where standing water is scarce. Nevertheless, like most other animals, uromastyx require drinking water to remain healthy.

Providing Drinking Water

Providing ample drinking water is imperative to the health of your uromastyx. Be sure to provide drinking water at least once each day, whether or not your lizard drinks any. This is especially important for young uromastyx, whose surface-to-volume ratio causes them to dehydrate more rapidly than adults do.

Providing drinking water to a uromastyx requires some ingenuity, as some individuals fail to recognize standing water for what it is. Instead of drinking from a water dish, most uromastyx prefer to drink droplets of water dripping from their bodies or the cage furniture.

The easiest way to provide water in this way is by misting the uromastyx and any plants inside the enclosure. The resulting water droplets will usually entice your uromastyx to lap them up greedily.

You can mist the cage with a hand-held misting bottle, a pressurized unit or an automated misting system. An inexpensive hand-held misting bottle usually suffices for those caring for a single uromastyx, while those maintaining several individuals often find the latter two options more efficient.

Ornate Uromastyx (Uromastyx ornata)

Nevertheless, some uromastyx (particularly adults) can learn to drink from a water dish, which makes maintenance much easier for the keeper. It is usually preferable to offer water for about 1 hour at a time before removing it until the next day. This prevents the animals from fouling the water and then ingesting bacteria or parasites.

Some keepers prefer to give their uromastyx dechlorinated or purified or spring water, but others simply offer tap water. Purified bottled water and spring water are typically safe for uromastyx, but distilled water should be avoided to prevent causing electrolyte imbalances.

It is wise to have tap water tested to ensure that heavy metals or other pollutants are not present before offering it to your uromastyx.

Soaking

In addition to providing drinking water, many keepers soak their uromastyx periodically in a tub of clean, lukewarm water. Soaking is a helpful tactic for the husbandry of many reptiles, even those who hail from arid habitats.

In addition to ensuring that your pet remains adequately hydrated, soaks help to remove dirt and encourage complete, problem-free sheds. It is not necessary to soak your lizard if it remains adequately hydrated, but most benefit from an occasional soak.

Soaks should last a maximum of about one hour, and be performed no more often than once per week.

Never make your lizard swim to keep its head above water. Only use enough to wet half of his body – but you can spray or pour water on his back during the soak.

Never leave your pet unattended while it is soaking. If your uromastyx defecates in the water, be sure to rinse him off with clean water before returning him to his cage.

Humidity

Uromastyx hail from habitats with a very low humidity for most of the year. Strive to keep their enclosure similarly dry to prevent your lizards from contracting respiratory infections and other problems.

As long as the habitat provides good ventilation, it will usually remain dry enough to keep your lizards healthy. Avoid leaving a large water dish in the cage at all times and be sure that the cage dries within a few hours of being misted.

Chapter 13: Interacting with Your Uromastyx

While uromastyx will never suffer from a lack of human interaction, most individuals will tolerate brief, gentle handling.

Handling Your Uromastyx

The very best way to handle your uromastyx is to try to slide your hand (or finger, in the case of small individuals) underneath his chin and gently begin lifting him up. This will normally cause your lizard to crawl into your hand voluntarily.

Hold your uromastyx gently in your hand, and place your thumb lightly on his back to prevent him from leaping off suddenly. Use care to avoid squeezing your uromastyx, as this will cause him to feel threatened, making him squirm to escape.

Never lift a uromastyx by the tail or the limbs, as this could lead to injuries.

Transporting Your Pet

Although you should strive to avoid any unnecessary travel with your lizard, circumstances often demand that you do (such as when your lizard becomes ill).

Strive to make the journey as stress-free as possible for your pet. This means protecting him from physical harm, as well as blocking as many stressful stimuli as possible.

The best type of container to use when transporting your uromastyx is a plastic storage box or small, screened cage.

Add several ventilation holes to plastic containers to provide suitable ventilation.

If the trip is to be brief, the added security, protection and thermal stability of a plastic storage box are generally preferable to the screened container. Conversely, the improved air exchange offered by a screened cage will prove beneficial on long journeys.

Place a few paper towels or some clean newspaper in the bottom of the box to absorb any fluids, should your lizard defecate or discharge urates. You can add a few plant cuttings to the cage to provide cover for your pet, but it is not strictly necessary.

Cover the outside of his transportation cage if you are not using an opaque container. This will prevent your pet from seeing the chaos occurring outside his container. Monitor your lizard regularly, but avoid constantly opening the container to take a peak. Checking up on your pet once every half-hour or so is more than sufficient.

Pay special attention to the enclosure temperatures while traveling. Use your digital thermometer to monitor the air temperatures inside the transportation container. Try to keep the temperatures in the low 80s Fahrenheit (26 to 29 degrees Celsius) so that your pet will remain comfortable. Use the air-conditioning or heater in your vehicle as needed to keep the animal within this range.

Do not jostle your pet unnecessarily and always use a gentle touch when moving the container. Never leave the container unattended.

Hygiene

Reptiles can carry *Salmonella* spp., *Escherichia coli* and several other zoonotic pathogens. Accordingly, it is imperative that you use good hygiene practices when handling reptiles.

Always wash your hands with soap and warm water each time you touch your pet, his habitat or the tools you use to care for him. Antibacterial soaps are preferred, but standard hand soap will suffice.

In addition to keeping your hands clean, you must also take steps to ensure *your* environment does not become contaminated with pathogens. In general, this means keeping your lizard and any of the tools and equipment you use to maintain his habitat separated from your belongings.

Establish a safe place for preparing his food, storing equipment and cleaning his habitat. Make sure these places are far from the places in which you prepare your food and personal effects. Never wash cages or tools in kitchens or bathrooms that are used by humans.

Always clean and sterilize any items that become contaminated by the germs from your lizard or his habitat.

Chapter 14: Common Health Concerns

Like many other lizards, uromastyx are remarkably hardy animals, who often remain healthy despite their keeper's mistakes. In fact, most illnesses that befall pet uromastyx result from improper husbandry, and are, therefore, entirely avoidable.

Nevertheless, like most other reptiles, uromastyx often fail to exhibit any symptoms that they are sick until they have reached an advanced state of illness. This means that prompt action is necessary at the first hint of a problem. Doing so provides your pet with the greatest chance of recovery.

While proper husbandry is solely in the domain of the keeper, and some minor injuries or illnesses can be treated at home, veterinary care is necessary for many health problems.

Finding a Suitable Vet

While any veterinarian – even one who specializes in dogs and cats – may be able to help you keep your pet happy, it is wise to find a veterinarian who specializes in treating reptiles. Such veterinarians are more likely to be familiar with your pet species and be familiar with the most current treatment standards for reptiles.

Some of the best places to begin your search for a reptile-oriented veterinarian include:

- Veterinary associations

- Local pet stores

- Local colleges and universities

It is always wise to develop a relationship with a qualified veterinarian before you need his or her services. This way, you will already know where to go in the event of an emergency, and your veterinarian will have developed some familiarity with your pet.

When to See the Vet

Most conscientious keepers will not hesitate to seek veterinary attention on behalf of their pet. However, veterinary care can be expensive for the keeper and stressful for the kept, so unnecessary visits are best avoided.

If you are in doubt, call or email your veterinarian and explain the problem. He or she can then advise you if the problem requires an office visit or not.

However, you must always seek prompt veterinary care if your pet exhibits any of the following signs or symptoms:

- Traumatic injuries, such as lacerations, burns, broken bones, cracked shells or puncture wounds

- Sores, ulcers, lumps or other deformations of the skin

- Intestinal disturbances that do not resolve within 48 hours

- Drastic change in behavior

- Inability to deposit eggs

Remember that reptiles are perfectly capable of feeling pain and suffering, so apply the golden rule: If you would appreciate medical care for an injury or illness, it is likely that your pet does as well.

Common Health Problems

The following are some of the most common health problems that afflict uromastyx. Be alert for any signs of the following maladies, and take steps to remedy the problem.

Respiratory Infections

Respiratory infections are some of the most common illnesses that afflict uromastyx and other captive reptiles.

The most common symptoms of respiratory infections are discharges from the nose or mouth; however, lethargy, inappetence and behavioral changes (such as basking more often than normal) may also accompany respiratory infections.

Myriad causes can lead to this type of illness, including communicable pathogens, as well as, ubiquitous, yet normally harmless, pathogens, which opportunistically infect stressed animals.

Your uromastyx may be able to fight off these infections without veterinary assistance, but it is wise to solicit your vet's opinion at the first sign of illness. Some respiratory infections can prove fatal and require immediate attention.

Your vet will likely obtain samples, send off the samples for laboratory testing and then interpret the results. Antibiotics or other medications may be prescribed to help your uromastyx recover, and your veterinarian will likely encourage you to keep the pet's stress level low and ensure his enclosure temperatures are ideal.

In fact, it is usually a good idea to raise the temperature of the basking spot upon first suspecting that your uromastyx is suffering from a respiratory infection. Elevated body temperatures (such as those that occur when mammals have fevers) help the pet's body to fight the infection, and many will bask for longer than normal when ill.

Metabolic Bone Disease

Metabolic bone disease (MBD) is a complicated phenomenon that befalls uromastyx who are provided with insufficient calcium or insufficient amounts of the active form of vitamin D (D3), which is necessary for calcium utilization.

A well-rounded, diverse diet with plenty of leafy green vegetables helps to ensure your pet receives enough calcium. Additionally, many keepers supplement their pet's food items with calcium powders. However, it is important to consult with your veterinarian to devise a suitable supplementation schedule, as providing too much calcium can be just as problematic as providing too little.

A balanced diet will provide your uromastyx with plenty of inactive vitamin D. To allow your pet to convert this into the active form, you must provide it with exposure to ultraviolet radiation (specifically UVB). This can be accomplished either by housing your uromastyx outdoors and allowing them to bask in natural sunlight, or by illuminating their enclosure with full spectrum lights that produce light in the UVB portion of the spectrum.

When deprived of proper lighting, the calcium levels in the pet's blood fall. This causes the lizard's body to draw calcium from his bones to rectify the problem.

As calcium is removed from the bones, they become soft and flexible, rather than hard and rigid. This can lead to broken bones or disfigurement, which can leave your uromastyx unable to eat, walk or swim.

Advanced cases of MBD are rarely treatable, and euthanasia is often the only humane option. However, when caught early and treated aggressively, some of the symptoms of the disease can be stopped. Accordingly, it is of the utmost importance to seek veterinary care at the first sign of MBD.

Parasites

Parasites are rare among captive-bred uromastyx, but poor husbandry can cause them to become a problem. Parasites rarely become problematic for wild uromastyx, unless they become injured, stressed or ill.

Most internal parasites cause intestinal problems, such as runny or watery stools, vomiting or decreased appetites. Your veterinarian can collect blood or stool samples from your uromastyx, analyze them to determine what parasites, if any, are present, and prescribe medications to clear the infestation. Often, multiple treatments are necessary to eradicate the parasites completely.

External parasites afflict uromastyx on occasion, usually in the form of ticks. Because some ticks carry dangerous diseases, you should have your veterinarian inspect any animal carrying the parasitic arthropods.

Anorexia

Uromastyx are normally ravenous eaters, who rarely pass up the chance to consume calories. However, they may refuse food if ill, if kept in suboptimal temperatures (including seasonally cool temperatures, such as occur during the winter) or are preoccupied with breeding.

Refusing a meal or two is not cause for alarm, but if your uromastyx refuses food for longer than this, be sure to review your husbandry practices. If the uromastyx continues to refuse food without an obvious reason for doing so, consult your veterinarian.

Injuries

Uromastyx can become injured in myriad ways, including battles with cagemates, overly zealous breeding attempts, or by sustaining burns from heaters. While uromastyx are likely to heal from most minor wounds without medical attention, serious wounds will necessitate veterinary assistance.

Your vet will likely clean the wound, make any repairs necessary and prescribe a course of antibiotics to help prevent infection. Be sure to keep the enclosure as clean as possible during the healing process.

Egg Binding

Egg binding occurs when a female is unable or unwilling to deposit her eggs in a timely fashion. If not treated promptly, death can result.

The primary symptoms of egg binding are similar to those that occur when a gravid uromastyx approaches parturition. Egg bound uromastyx may dig to create an egg chamber or attempt to escape their enclosure. However, unlike uromastyx who will deposit eggs normally, egg bound uromastyx continue to exhibit these symptoms without producing a clutch of eggs.

As long as you are expecting your uromastyx to lay eggs, you can easily monitor her behavior and act quickly if she experiences problems. However, if you are not anticipating a clutch, this type of problem can catch you by surprise.

Prolapse

Prolapses occur when a uromastyx' intestines protrude from its vent. This is an emergency situation that requires prompt treatment. Fortunately, intestinal prolapse is not terribly common among uromastyx.

You will need to take the animal to the veterinarian, who will attempt to re-insert the intestinal sections. Sometimes sutures will be necessary to keep the intestines in place while the muscles regain their tone.

Try to keep the exposed tissue damp, clean and protected while traveling to the vet. It is likely that this problem is very painful for the animal, so try to keep its stress level low during the process.

Quarantine

Quarantine is the practice of isolating animals to prevent them from transferring diseases between themselves.

If you have no other pet reptiles (particularly other uromastyx), quarantine is unnecessary. However, if you already maintain other uromastyx you must provide all new acquisitions with a separate enclosure.

At a minimum, quarantine all new acquisitions for 30 days. However, it is wiser still to extend the quarantine period for 60 to 90 days, to give yourself a better chance of discovering any illness present before exposing your colony to new, potentially sick, animals. Professional zoological institutions often quarantine animals for six months to a year. In fact, some zoos keep their animals in a state of perpetual quarantine.

Chapter 15: Breeding Uromastyx

Many – if not most – uromastyx keepers are eventually bitten by the captive breeding bug. Determined to produce a clutch of adorable hatchlings, these keepers acquire specimens of each sex and begin waiting for eggs.

This is a natural progression for keepers, and, when carried out in a responsible fashion, breeding can be beneficial for the species, as captive breeding projects help alleviate pressure on wild populations.

However, irresponsible breeders often cause serious problems for the hobby.

Such breeders often set out with the explicit goal of profiting from their uromastyx, rather than enjoying their pets in their own right. This ensures failure for the vast majority of people that try to breed uromastyx for profit.

Pre-Breeding Considerations

Before you set out to breed uromastyx, consider the decision carefully. Unfortunately, few keepers realize the implications of breeding their uromastyx before they set out to do so.

Ask yourself if you will be able to:

- Provide adequate care for a pair of adult uromastyx

- Provide the proper care for the female while gravid

- Afford emergency veterinary services if necessary

- Incubate the eggs in some type of incubator

- Provide housing for the hatchlings

- Provide food for the hatchlings

- Dedicate the time to caring for the hatchlings

- Find new homes for the hatchlings

- If you cannot answer each of these questions affirmatively, you are not in a position to breed uromastyx responsibly.

Legal Issues

Before deciding to breed uromastyx, you must investigate the relevant laws in your area. Some municipalities require uromastyx breeders to obtain licenses, insurance and permits, although others do not.

Sexing Uromastyx

Adult uromastyx exhibit a few secondary sexual characteristics that help distinguish males from females. Males usually reach larger sizes than females do and occasionally possess larger heads. Males also tend to have more prominent femoral pores than females do, when present.

However, the most definitive clues can be found on the underside of your uromastyx' tail base. Begin by resting your lizard on your palm, with its head facing away from you. Gently grip your lizard's tail and arch it over the back. If it is a male, you should be able to see its hemipenes on both sides of the tail, right behind the vent. Females, by contrast, have no such bulges. Sometimes it is easiest to see the bulges by gently twisting the tail from side to side while looking for the bulges.

Hemipenal bulges are the only reliable way of sexing you uromastyx, but it is much more difficult to distinguish between the sexes when the animals are young. However, it becomes pretty easy to sex them by the time they are about 12 weeks of age. Experienced breeders can often discern a uromastyx' sex long before this.

Pre-Breeding Conditioning

Breeding reptiles always entails risk, so it is wise to refrain from breeding any animals that are not in excellent health. Breeding is especially stressful for female uromastyx, who must withstand potential injuries during mating, and produce numerous, nutrient-rich eggs.

Animals slated for breeding trials must have excellent body weight, but obesity is to be avoided, as it is associated with reproductive problems. Ensure that the lizards are appropriately hydrated, and are free of parasites, infections and injuries.

Cycling

Cycling is the terms used to describe the climactic changes keepers impose upon their animals. These changes are intended to mimic the natural seasonal changes in an animal's natural habitat.

Uromastyx keepers seeking to breed their animals often simulate winter conditions by reducing the enclosure temperatures and providing fewer hours of lighting for a period of 1 to 3 months. Generally, by shifting from 12 to 14 hours of light, cycling regimens call for only 4 to 6 hours of light each day. When the lights are off, the cage temperatures are allowed to fall to the ambient temperature of the room.

These changes may not be strictly necessary for stimulating uromastyx to breed, but it is generally beneficial for breeding efforts. Nevertheless, some breeders have had success without using a cycling regimen at all.

It is important to reduce the temperatures and photoperiod gradually to avoid stressing the animals. Additionally, food should be withheld during the cycling period. Provide water to the animals periodically to avoid dehydration.

At the end of the cycling period, begin restoring the lights and temperatures to their normal level. Begin feeding the animals as soon as they will start eating. It is important that they feed well before breeding trials commence.

Breeding Trials

Once the uromastyx have had a few days to feed following cycling, breeding trials can begin.

If you maintain the animals together all year long, copulations will likely occur without any additional effort on your part. If you keep the animals separately for most of the year, this is the time to introduce them to each other.

Most breeders using this method introduce males into the cages of their female counterparts, but the opposite strategy can be just as effective.

Copulation may begin almost immediately, or it may take several hours to occur. The pair may copulate only once, or they may copulate several times over many days. It is usually wise to house the pair together for several days (if they are not permanent cagemates), to allow for multiple copulations, thereby helping to ensure good fertility.

Care of the Gravid Female

With some luck, the female will become gravid (pregnant) shortly after the animals have bred. Isolate the female once she begins displaying such symptoms. This will help keep her stress level low and allow you to provide better care for her.

Provide gravid females with a suitable egg-deposition chamber. A plastic storage container or cat litter pan makes a suitable chamber. Experienced breeders often transfer females to egg chambers outside of their cages shortly before oviposition occurs, but this only introduces unnecessary complexity to the process that novices are wise to avoid – just place the container inside the female's enclosure and let her find it.

Fill the chamber about two-thirds full with very slightly damp soil and pack it gently into place. The soil must not be wet, but it must have enough moisture to allow the lizard to create a stable tunnel and egg chamber. As a rule of thumb, you should be able to compress the soil into a clump when you squeeze it in your hand, without causing any water to trickle out.

Near the end of the gestation, which typically lasts about three to four weeks, females develop very plump abdomens. In some cases, the faint outline of eggs can be seen through the abdominal wall.

Do not handle gravid females unless absolutely necessary, and try to keep their stress level as low as possible.

Egg Deposition

If the female finds the egg chamber satisfactory, she will crawl into the container and dig a small tunnel that ends in an enlarged chamber. She will then turn around and deposit 6 to 25 eggs. After she has completed the process, she will climb back out of the tunnel and cover it completely.

It is a good idea to mist her thoroughly at this time, so she can rehydrate. Misting her will also help to rinse the dirt off her.

If the female does not find the egg chamber to her liking, she may dig multiple tunnels or simply crawl back out of the egg chamber without depositing her eggs. This can be problematic, as retained eggs represent a very serious health problem.

Try to adjust the substrate in the egg chamber with hopes that she will try again and find your changes helpful. You may need to add water to the substrate or dry out the substrate by mixing in fresh, dry soil.

Always observe gravid uromastyx carefully for signs that suggest they are unable to deposit their eggs. For example, egg-bound females may pace back and forth in the cage, dig multiple burrows without depositing eggs or simply become lethargic. If your female displays these signs, you must take her to your veterinarian without delay.

Egg binding is a serious medical condition that can become fatal very quickly. However, with prompt attention, your vet may be able to administer medications which will help her deposit eggs. If that fails to have the desired effect, your vet may perform surgery on the female, to remove the eggs from her body. Such eggs are highly unlikely to hatch, but this will usually save the life of your female. However, she may be rendered unable to breed by such operations.

Retrieving the Eggs

Once the female has deposited her eggs and you have ensured she is rehydrated and in good health, begin excavating the tunnel. Use a gentle touch and take care not to damage the eggs.

Avoid rotating the eggs while removing and transferring them to the egg chamber. It is often helpful to mark the top of each egg with a graphite pencil. This way, you can be sure to place them in the same orientation in which they settled into the egg mass.

Separate any eggs that come apart easily, but never use excessive force when doing so. If a cluster of eggs will not separate easily, they should be left attached to each other and incubated as they are.

Place the eggs in a deli cup or plastic food container, half-filled with slightly dampened vermiculite (most keepers use a 1:1 ratio of vermiculite to water, by weight). When in doubt, subject the vermiculite to the same test used for the egg deposition substrate – it should clump when compressed, but not release any water.

Bury the eggs halfway into the vermiculite and close the container. Try to space the eggs so that none are in direct contact with any others.

Egg Incubation

Uromastyx eggs are fairly easy to incubate. You can purchase a commercially produced incubator or construct your own. Most any incubator designed for use with reptile eggs will suffice, but it is wise to test the unit and ensure it holds consistent temperatures before you are faced with eggs.

You can make your own incubator by filling a 10-gallon aquarium with a few inches of water. Place an aquarium heater in the water, and set the thermostat at the desired temperature. Place a brick in the water and rest the egg chamber on top of the brick. Cover the aquarium with a glass top to keep the heat and moisture contained.

Set your incubator to about 92 degrees Fahrenheit (33 degrees Celsius) for the duration of the incubation time. The young will usually begin hatching after 60 to 85 days.

Individual eggs may progress at slightly different rates, so hatchlings may emerge from the clutch over the course of a period of several days. Many of the hatchlings will remain in their egg for 24 hours or so, while they absorb the remainder of their egg yolk. Do not attempt to remove the lizards from their eggs – allow them to exit on their own.

The Incubator

You can either purchase a commercially produced incubator or construct your own. However, most beginning breeders are better served by purchasing a commercial incubator than making their own.

Commercial Incubators

Commercial egg incubators come in myriad styles and sizes. Some of the most popular models are similar to those used to incubate poultry eggs (these are often available for purchase from livestock supply retailers).

These incubators are constructed from a large foam box, fitted with a heating element and thermostat. Some models feature a fan for circulating air; while helpful for maintaining a uniform thermal environment, models that lack these fans are acceptable.

You can place an incubation medium directly in the bottom of these types of incubators, although it is preferable to place the media (and eggs) inside small plastic storage boxes, which are then placed inside the incubator.

These incubators are usually affordable and easy to use, although their foam-based construction makes them less durable than most premium incubators are.

Other incubators are constructed from metal or plastic boxes; feature a clear door, an enclosed heating element and a thermostat. Some units also feature a backup thermostat, which can provide some additional protection in case the primary thermostat fails.

These types of incubators usually outperform economy, foam-based models, but they also bear higher price tags. Either style will work, but, if you plan to breed lizards for many years, premium models usually present the best option.

Homemade Incubators

Although incubators can be constructed in a variety of ways, using many different materials and designs, two basic designs are most common.

The first type of homemade incubator consists of a plastic, glass or wood box, and a simple heat source, such as a piece of heat tape or a low-wattage heat lamp. The heating source must be attached to a thermostat to keep the temperatures consistent. A thermometer is also necessary for monitoring the temperatures of the incubator.

Some keepers make these types of incubators from wood, while others prefer plastic or foam. Although glass is a poor insulator, aquariums often serve as acceptable incubators; however, you must purchase or construct a solid top to retain heat.

Place a brick on the bottom of the incubator, and place the egg box on top of the brick, so that the eggs are not resting directly on the heat tape. The brick will also provide thermal mass to the incubator, which will help maintain a more consistent temperature.

The other popular incubator design adds a quantity of water to the design to help maintain consistent temperatures and a higher humidity. To build such a unit, begin with an aquarium fitted with a glass or plastic lid.

Place a brick in the bottom of the aquarium and add about two gallons of water to the aquarium; ideally, the water level should stop right below the top of the brick.

Add an aquarium heater to the water and set the thermostat to the desired temperature. Place the egg box on the brick, insert a temperature probe into the egg box and cover the aquarium with the lid (you may need to purchase a lid designed to allow the cords to pass through it).

This type of incubator works by heating the water, which will in turn heat the air inside the incubator, which will heat the eggs. Although it can take several days of repeated adjustments to get these types of incubators set to the exact temperature you would like, they are very stable once established.

Neonatal Husbandry

Once the young begin hatching from their eggs, you can remove them from the egg box and place them in a small cage or "nursery." Do not attempt to remove any hatchlings from their eggs. If any of the young emerge with their yolk sacs still attached, leave them in the egg box until they have absorbed the yolk.

A 20-gallon aquarium with a bare floor and a screened lid makes a satisfactory nursery. Place several small hides in the tank to provide the young with some form of cover.

Mist the young several times per day and keep the temperatures at about 86 degrees Fahrenheit (30 degrees Celsius). You can initiate feeding trials within a day or two, but do not be surprised if the young lizards do not begin eating for several days.

Keep the young in the nursery until they begin feeding regularly. At this point, you can begin breaking them into small groups and placing them in their permanent homes.

Chapter 16: Further Reading

Never stop learning more about your new pet's natural history, biology and captive care. This is the only way to ensure that you are providing your new uromastyx with the highest quality of life possible.

It's always more fun to watch your uromastyx than read about him, but by accumulating more knowledge, you'll be better able to provide him with a high quality of life.

Books

Bookstores and online book retailers offer a treasure trove of information that will advance your quest for knowledge. While books represent an additional cost involved in reptile care, you can consider it an investment in your pet's well-being. Your local library may also carry some books about uromastyx, which you can borrow for no charge.

University libraries are a great place for finding old, obscure or academically oriented books about uromastyx. You may not be allowed to borrow these books if you are not a student, but you can view and read them at the library.

Herpetology: An Introductory Biology of Amphibians and Reptiles
By Laurie J. Vitt, Janalee P. Caldwell
Top of Form
Bottom of Form
Academic Press, 2013

Understanding Reptile Parasites: A Basic Manual for Herpetoculturists & Veterinarians
By Roger Klingenberg D.V.M.

Advanced Vivarium Systems, 1997
Infectious Diseases and Pathology of Reptiles: Color Atlas and Text
Elliott Jacobson
CRC Press

Designer Reptiles and Amphibians
Richard D. Bartlett, Patricia Bartlett
Barron's Educational Series

Magazines

Because magazines are typically published monthly or bi-monthly, they occasionally offer more up-to-date information than books do. Magazine articles are obviously not as comprehensive as books typically are, but they still have considerable value.

Reptiles Magazine
www.reptilesmagazine.com/
Covering reptiles commonly kept in captivity.

Practical Reptile Keeping
http://www.practicalreptilekeeping.co.uk/
Practical Reptile Keeping is a popular publication aimed at beginning and advanced hobbies. Topics include the care and maintenance of popular reptiles as well as information on wild reptiles.

Websites

The internet has made it much easier to find information about reptiles than it has ever been.

However, you must use discretion when deciding which websites to trust. While knowledgeable breeders, keepers and academics operate some websites, many who maintain reptile-oriented websites lack the same dedication to scientific rigor.

Anyone with a computer and internet connection can launch a website and say virtually anything they want about uromastyx. Accordingly, as with all other research, consider the source of the information before making any husbandry decisions.

The Reptile Report
www.thereptilereport.com/
The Reptile Report is a news-aggregating website that accumulates interesting stories and features about reptiles from around the world.

Kingsnake.com
www.kingsnake.com
After starting as a small website for gray-banded kingsnake enthusiasts, Kingsnake.com has become one of the largest reptile-oriented portals in the hobby. The site features classified advertisements, a breeder directory, message forums and other resources.

The Vivarium and Aquarium News
www.vivariumnews.com/
The online version of the former print publication, The Vivarium and Aquarium News provides in-depth coverage of different reptiles and amphibians in a captive and wild context.

Journals
Journals are the primary place professional scientists turn when they need to learn about uromastyx. While they may

not make light reading, hobbyists stand to learn a great deal from journals.

Herpetologica
www.hljournals.org/
Published by The Herpetologists' League, Herpetologica, and its companion publication, Herpetological Monographs cover all aspects of reptile and amphibian research.

Journal of Herpetology
www.ssarherps.org/
Produced by the Society for the Study of Reptiles and Amphibians, the Journal of Herpetology is a peer-reviewed publication covering a variety of reptile-related topics.

Copeia
www.asihcopeiaonline.org/
Copeia is published by the American Society of Ichthyologists and Herpetologists. A peer-reviewed journal, Copeia covers all aspects of the biology of reptiles, amphibians and fish.

Nature
www.nature.com/
Although Nature covers all aspects of the natural world, many issues contain information that uromastyx enthusiasts are sure to find interesting.

Supplies
You can obtain most of what you need to maintain uromastyx through your local pet store, big-box retailer or hardware store, but online retailers offer another option.

Just be sure that you consider the shipping costs for any purchase, to ensure you aren't "saving" yourself a few dollars on the product, yet spending several more dollars to get the product delivered.

Big Apple Pet Supply
http://www.bigappleherp.com
Big Apple Pet Supply carries most common husbandry equipment, including heating devices, water dishes and substrates.

LLLReptile
http://www.lllreptile.com
LLL Reptile carries a wide variety of husbandry tools, heating devices, lighting products and more.

Doctors Foster and Smith
http://www.drsfostersmith.com
Foster and Smith is a veterinarian-owned retailer that supplies husbandry-related items to pet keepers.

Support Organizations
Sometimes, the best way to learn about uromastyx is to reach out to other keepers and breeders. Check out these organizations, and search for others in your geographic area.

The National Reptile & Amphibian Advisory Council
http://www.nraac.org/
The National Reptile & Amphibian Advisory Council seeks to educate the hobbyists, legislators and the public about reptile and amphibian related issues.

American Veterinary Medical Association
www.avma.org

The AVMA is a good place for Americans to turn if you are having trouble finding a suitable reptile veterinarian.

The World Veterinary Association
http://www.worldvet.org/
The World Veterinary Association is a good resource for finding suitable reptile veterinarians worldwide.

References

al, T. M. (2007). On the Phylogeny and Taxonomy of the Genus Uromastyx Merrem, 1820 (Reptilia: Squamata: Agamidae: Uromastycinae) – Resurrection of the Genus Saara Gray, 1845. *Bonner Zoologische Beiträge*.

Anderson, S. P. (2003). The Phylogenetic Definition of Reptilia. *Systematic Biology*.

Evans, D. S. (2003). *Uromastyx hardwickii, Indian Spiny-tailed Lizard*. Retrieved from Digimorph: http://digimorph.org/specimens/Uromastyx_hardwicki i/

Joger, U. (. (1996). Analysis of the herpetofauna of the Republic of Mali. Annotated inventory, with a description of a new Uromastyx (Sauria: Agamidae) [1996]. *FAO*.

KUMAZAWA, S. A. (2005). Mitochondrial DNA sequences of the Afro-Arabian spiny-tailed lizards (genus Uromastyx; family Agamidae): phylogenetic analyses and evolution of gene arrangements. *Biological Journal of the Linnean Society*.

M.F.Hussein, N. R. (1978). Effect of seasonal variation on lymphoid tissues of the lizards, Mabuya quinquetaeniata licht. and Uromastyx aegyptia forsk. *Developmental & Comparative Immunology*.

Poole, J. S. (1973). The dentition and dental tissues of the agamid lizard, Uromastyx. *Journal of Zoology*.

W. J. Foley, A. B. (1992). Microbial digestion in the herbivorous lizard Uromastyx aegyptius (Agamidae). *Journal of Zoology*.

William E Cooper, J. (2000). Chemosensory discrimination of plant and animal foods by the omnivorous iguanian lizard Pogona vitticeps. *Canadian Journal of Zoology.*

Index

Made in the USA
Las Vegas, NV
13 December 2023

82703688R00069